"Thank goodness Emma Lou writes things down. In her poetry or prose she has the ability to make us laugh and likewise to cry but always the unique ability to make us understand life a little better. I did not know Emma Lou until my college days, but somehow she always stood out in my life as a role model. Whether it was skiing, tennis, speaking, or writing, she excelled. She established a pattern that told all of us that were a few years younger, that it was possible to put your family first, but still find remarkable opportunities to reach out and make a difference in the world."

—Olene S. Walker, first woman governor of Utah

"In view of the terrifying event with which it begins, it is a wonderful surprise to find the tremendous joy behind this book. It is everywhere suffused with Emma Lou Thayne's astonishing energy and capacity for love. She has found many lives inside herself, and teaches us to rejoice in that."

—Henry Taylor, Pulitzer Prize winner, *The Flying Change*

"I think this book is Emma Lou's tour de force. I read it in two sittings, resenting any interruption. I couldn't put it down. Her 'voice' and spirit and visual poetic nature reached my heart and spirit, as if apart from my mind. The depth of her spirituality and belief in the goodness of people inspire me toward 'childness.'"

—Stephen R. Covey, author, *The 7 Habits of Highly Effective People*

THE
PLACE
OF KNOWING

THE PLACE OF KNOWING

A Spiritual Autobiography

EMMA LOU WARNER THAYNE

Published by iUniverse
Bloomington, Indiana

The views expressed in this work are solely those of the author and do not necessarily reflect the views of the publisher, and the publisher hereby disclaims any responsibility for them.

iUniverse books may be ordered through booksellers or by contacting:

iUniverse
1663 Liberty Drive
Bloomington, IN 47403
www.iuniverse.com
1-800-Authors (1-800-288-4677)

Because of the dynamic nature of the Internet, any Web addresses or links contained in this book may have changed since publication and may no longer be valid. The views expressed in this work are solely those of the author and do not necessarily reflect the views of the publisher, and the publisher hereby disclaims any responsibility for them.

Any people depicted in stock imagery provided by Thinkstock are models, and such images are being used for illustrative purposes only.

Certain stock imagery © Thinkstock.

Book designer/cover designer, Maralee Nelson
www.mGraphicDesign.com

ISBN: 978-1-4502-8527-8 (sc)
ISBN: 978-1-4502-8526-1 (hc)
ISBN: 978-1-4502-8525-4 (ebook)

Library of Congress Control Number: 2011900247

Printed in the United States of America

iUniverse rev. date: 01/10/2011

A VALENTINE FOR MEL

How much difference that we love?
Do you, knotted with concerns, need me
more for a head rub or for turning down the furnace
or for explaining silence and its offerings
or for playfulness, the unbelievably enormous attractions
or for seeing that things happen?

Waiting as we are today for four more days
before we know why blood tests highlight
a prostate like your yellow felt tip on a page of scripture,
much as love would like, I cannot be with you
on the inside, any more than from this little distance
you can feel the spring that wakes in me,
your wife watching the snow melt in the rain
and listening for your sweet whistle of arrival
cradling me as I would cradle you
in the well supported shape you have worried
and loved into our life.

My one hand holding tight to yours
I will come celebrate with you
that so far what has tried to kill us, either one,
has not succeeded. And that for each other
nothing ever will.

| CONTENTS |

Foreword   ix

Preface   xi

Acknowledgments   xiii

Chapter 1 | Journey to the Place of Knowing   1

Chapter 2 | Pillars and Stars—to Know and Tell   31

Chapter 3 | Reverence for Life—From Birth to Death and Beyond   73

Chapter 4 | Living with the Ineffable—in Sleep, Solitude, and Serenity   89

Chapter 5 | Language of the Heart   109

Chapter 6 | Where Can I Turn for Peace?   149

Chapter 7 | The Stations of the Cross   189

Chapter 8 | Healers   205

Chapter 9 | The Ineffable Shared   223

Chapter 10 | On Paying Attention   235

Epilogue   251

Glossary   253

FOREWORD

Emma Lou Thayne once said to me, "To make an event a reality, I have to write it down." Thank goodness Emma Lou writes things down. In her poetry or prose, she has the ability to make us laugh and likewise to cry but always the unique ability to make us understand life a little better.

In this book, she has shared many of her adventures and the deep commitment she has to living life to the maximum. She gives us her sense of beauty in nature, learning, community responsibility, and building lasting friendships. She gives us the opportunity to find that all of our lives have trials and tribulations but these trials can become growing experiences that in the long run enrich our understanding and reverence for life. Indeed, this is a book that should inspire all of us to reach out in friendship to others and to embrace new experiences. Especially for women, it outlines the potential we all have for expanding our horizons and our ability to influence policies and events, not only in our own neighborhoods and communities, but also on a global level.

Emma Lou has captured in this book what our friend Lowell Bennion meant when he talked about the responsibility we have in life of both vertically connecting to God and the spiritual, and horizontally connecting to and caring for other people. This book brings to our consciousness how each individual, regardless of social, economic, or religious beliefs, is someone who adds a richness of spirit and dignity to the pattern of our lives.

I did not know Emma Lou until my college days, but somehow she always stood out in my life as a role model. Whether it was in skiing, tennis, speaking, or writing, she excelled. She established a pattern that told all of us that were a few years younger, that it was possible to put your family first, but still find remarkable opportunities to reach out and make a difference in the world.

There is a reason Emma Lou is requested to speak at many funerals: among all the outstanding talents she has, perhaps the greatest is being a true and loyal friend. I hope that readers of this book share with me the understanding that we have looked into the heart and soul of a truly remarkable woman. How fortunate I have been to be able to call Emma Lou Thayne a friend and soul mate.

—Olene S. Walker, first woman governor of Utah

PREFACE

The word "mystic" is as dangerous as the word "poet," if only because both words are so vulnerable to misunderstanding and abuse. When we describe someone as a "poet" or a "mystic," we generally mean it as a warning—here is someone whose head is in the clouds and who can't get places on time. Someone we admire, or profess to admire, if we hold a romantic, sentimental view of either poetry or religion. But we wouldn't want our child to marry one, let alone become one.

—Kathleen Norris

To suggest that a trustworthy Mormon matriarch could also be a mystic may seem a total contradiction in terms. Here is the story of why it is not.

I died and came back. This book began with trying to decipher my death experience and return, now decades ago. Over those years the story has gestated under everything else I was writing and has become a memoir. At various stages it has been titled *Soul Talk, The*

Mystic Life of a Mormon Matriarch, and *The Wheel of Where*; now it is born as *The Place of Knowing*.

Knowing is a process, not an arrival. And deciphering the knowing has been as unpredictable as spring runoff after deep snow in a time of drought. Nothing could have ever prepared me for what I came to know—except maybe living to be eighty-six. At any age, life has to be lived before we can know what it is. Here, I've come alive to my childhood and growing up. I also have new acquaintance with my adulthood, where my dear dead almost outnumber the living, and both continue to enliven me. In reliving these parts of my life and death, I have learned even more to applaud any goodness in the world.

Moments of light have emerged as epiphanies. Since my experience with death, I have found that God, angels, my private muse, and the power of unseen connections have led and informed me, both by day and by night, to be welcomed just before waking. *Webster* defines mystic as "the experience of the inner light."

This book about death and life is also a love story—vertically with the divine, horizontally with the earthly. Even in my most calamitous times, love has been elemental. Days rich in necessary responsibility and roles, yet full of adventure and people, have opened into nights equally rich in clarifications and arrivals. None of this offering has come from study or effort, yet none of it could I ever have come to on my own.

Mary Oliver said, "Light is an invitation to happiness, and that happiness, when it's done right, is a kind of holiness." That astonishing light of our own being and that of others can be trusted to go on shining. This book is not to *explain* as much as to *expand* that trust.

As that Mormon matriarch still grounded in the pioneer devotion of my progenitors and many loved ones, I invite you to join in my mystic journey, to abide and grow with me in the place of no fear, of great affection and light, accessible—the way it is.

—Emma Lou Warner Thayne

ACKNOWLEDGMENTS

I am grateful beyond expression

To Jim and Dr. Louis Morales for saving my face and bringing me back to life.

To readers and expert suggesters through eighteen years of the story finding its way: Laurel, DeAnn, Linda, Lavina, Lisa, Sharon, Dawn A., Janice, and Helen.

To Marie, my technological guru, advisor, and one of my literary executors.

To Dawn M. for two years of loving expertise in saving my manuscript from abandonment and me from discouragement.

To Edith W. for a final rescue and edit.

To Jennifer for carrying the manuscript across the finish line.

To Alex, my publicist.

To friends with confidence and cheering: Ann and Greg of the Marriott Library, Shauna, June, Barbara, Colleen; to members of Soul Talk, Verbal Events, Laurels, peace groups, the Fini paintings committee, the Bennion study group; and to my board and ward friends and bishops.

To my daughters Becky, Rinda, Shelley, Dinny, and Megan for their love in making sure I tell of prices to pay for a full life and that gifts of the spirit are available to anyone.

To my sons-in-law, "P," Mike, Ed, and Brent for being there to talk with and my grandchildren for smiling with their Grandma Grey.

To mystical inspiration from Rachel, Brent, and Camille, along with healing sustenance by Barbara and Michelle.

To Peggy and Parry for a place and encouragement to write.

To Mel for unfailing love and support in understanding and even in not understanding.

To Mother and Father, my brothers and sisters-in-law, and generations before and after me for giving their whole-hearted acceptance in my riding the wild horse.

To the divine that has inspired it all.

———

CHAPTER 1

JOURNEY TO
THE PLACE
OF KNOWING

An exaltation of joy . . . even more beautiful than anything in a dream.

—Madeleine L'Engle

Things happen. Early in the world you travel into them. One day you rise without prayer in a far camp and silently hurry away. Having slept under stars and still breathing the greyed fire, who would take time to suppose this the middle of a lifetime?

The day I died, my son-in-law Jim and I had to leave camp early that Saturday morning, June 28, 1986. He needed to be at the hospital where he was chief resident in plastic surgery, and I wanted to be back to help a good friend with the announcement party at noon for her daughter's wedding. Leaving our loved ones asleep, we drove my husband Mel's new Taurus. With Jim at the wheel, we laughed as I read from the car's manual about what knob or button would activate what magic—such as how many miles we were getting or how far before we ran out of gas. Luckily, I was looking down while I read.

Without warning came the crash. A six-pound rod, like a tire iron with an elbow in it, somehow airborne, smashed through the windshield into my face. It missed my right eye by a hair and lodged in the rear window of the car.

Jim didn't see the iron bar until it struck me—when he saw my head fly back and then forward. Without a seat belt, he said later, my body would have recoiled back through the fractured windshield. "What hit me?" I asked him, my hand at my temple full of blood, glass in my eye. That blood! Jim looked at me, then toward the back of the car. "You'll never believe what hit you, Grey," I heard him say. "It's huge! A piece of iron as long as my arm, and it's stuck in the back window." I guess I asked him to give me his T-shirt for the blood. He pulled onto the shoulder of the highway, stopped, stripped off his shirt, and pressed it against my temple and eye.

What must it have felt like to him, specializing in plastic surgery, knowing what he did about facial and head injuries? How frightened was he? He'd been my pal, my partner on the tennis court. He loved our daughter and their children. We'd planned to write a mystery novel about a burn patient uncompromisingly wanting his fingerprints changed. Hoping for a patrolman, Jim turned on the flashers and drove ninety miles an hour to his hospital.

Somewhere, I had lost track of myself. If there was anything happening, it was someone else's story. I lost all feeling. There was no present, no past, no future—only a grey miasma of nothing crucial, nothing needing my attention. Disbelief filled me. What had smashed the windshield and my face? Did it matter? Numb, without pain or caring, I felt Jim speeding through traffic to the hospital. How long it took was of no concern. Strangely, I think I felt invulnerable, as if what had happened were not part of my life.

Outside of the emergency room, I was vaguely aware as attendants pushed on me here, there—testing reflexes, asking questions of Jim, of me. They put a collar on my neck, laid me on a stretcher, and rushed me to x-ray. I felt nothing as doctors tried to clean glass out of my eye. Windshield splinters covered me. Splinters from my smashed sunglasses were in my eye as well. I was blank, a nonentity—I felt only distance and almost indifference.

The x-rays would show eight fractures, a broken jaw, and six teeth killed. My eyeball would have to be moved to allow for repair of the socket. Concussion—what else to my brain? No one should have survived, the police officers, doctors, staff, and reporters said then.

But I thought I hadn't even lost consciousness.

Uncharacteristically, my family were all unavailable, either back at camp or otherwise out of town. Shelley, Paul, and their three children had just moved to Alameda, California. Dinny and Mike were running a summer tennis camp in Ojai, California, for which Megan had left only the week before to be an assistant instructor in tennis and swimming. Jim was meeting with his chief of surgery, Dr. Louis Morales, to discuss what needed to happen for me. I lay alone in some white room, waiting—but not waiting.

Out of the dim, our daughter Becky mysteriously appeared, almost vaporous. Jim had found her family where I had told him they were weekending, at Snowbird resort twenty miles away. As any one of my five daughters would have done, she took my hand. I thought she was crying. Her love palpable, she was reality—but not reality. It would be weeks before I could reenter myself, let alone my world. Where I was, there was no such thing as emotion. Seven months later, I would write:

To you nothing here is immediate, crucial, in the least attractive.

No expecting beyond hours of x-rays, stitches, shots, ice.

All that time returning, you vague about familiar hands,
tangled in your head, the blow to trace, surely someone else's story.

Because of the swelling, Dr. Morales could not operate that day. All he could do was stitch me up and wait until ice and rest could reduce the purple protrusion by my eye and over my temple. I agreed with Jim, almost without thought, not to let our family who were still camping know about the accident. What good? They'd be back in the afternoon, driving without having to worry about me. Despite my serious condition, Jim, my closest advisor, knew I would want to be home to wait out my time before surgery. He knew how critical the familiar would be to my recovery from trauma. He took me home via my own eye doctor who, with the caring expertise I was used to, gently removed the final shards of glass from my eye. I never cried. I was not afraid. I felt nothing, not even great pain. Someone else occupied my skin.

Five hours later, Mel came into our bedroom not knowing what had happened, only that there had been an accident. I lay on a treasured pillow in some dim region, wanting nothing. His hand went to his mouth and he sobbed. Until then, I had no idea of how I looked. Jim had told Rinda at the door. She came to the bed and, like Becky, took my hand and said, "You'll be OK, Mother." Then she and Becky called my brothers and friends to say that I'd had a small accident. One by one they came to me, bringing their individual looks of veiled dismay. Jim took a picture of me lying there with the rusted iron rod beside me, as long as from my head to my hips. He also took a picture of the smashed slit in the windshield, crackles around it, looking like a great glass eye peering into and out of the passenger seat of the car.

Two days later, I scrawled in the journal I could not read, "All I've been saying since 7:30 Sat. morning is 'thank you. Thank you. Another chance, Lulie, take it & run!'"

Surgery came four days after the accident, scheduled in a rush before the Fourth of July weekend when Dr. Morales would be out of town. He asked for a picture of the right side of my face before the injury. He would restore me, but to what? Would that it could be Ingrid Bergman! But then again, how I might look seemed almost incidental to how much I wanted my eye back for seeing, or my brain for thinking. My brother Homer, who was a doctor, had long ago explained to me that in a concussion the brain is like an egg in a teacup. With a blow the cup can appear intact even though the egg has been shattered. I wanted my shattered head back in one piece.

I had always looked for divine help through my faith in healing; I'd looked for divine help in anything actually—whether taking an exam or talking to someone in trouble. But this situation seemed different. Words and ideas were lost in a fog of no feeling. Prayer had always been as natural as breathing, but I felt separated even from that. Mother and Father led us in blessings on our food and entreaties for help, even to play our best in a game or tournament. As adults, when we were flying as my three brothers and I often were, Mother was "working on the weather," and we all had stories of miraculous breaking up of storms.

In 1924, when I was a month old, my father had stood in a circle of priesthood bearers in front of the congregation I was born into to give me a name and a blessing. That event is recorded in the cornerstone of the then-new Highland Park Ward, where I was the first baby to be christened. I can remember still, when I was four and had both measles and whooping cough long before medicines to cure either, there were signs in our front window alerting others to the highly contagious diseases in our home. I must have been dangerously ill. It was time for a blessing.

I can still feel the kitchen stool I sat on in front of the radiator in the living room to stay warm. My father and an adored uncle put their big hands on my head. They felt like a heavy capful of magic. My scalp still rises thinking about it. I heard my father's voice being very serious, and he was crying—most of the time he laughed with us so I felt his seriousness down my neck and into my shoulders. I remember being carried by my father back upstairs to the bed I shared with my grandmother, expecting for sure to be back in first grade the next day where the school nurse would take my temperature and let me stay. Only the blessing part is still clear, but I know I didn't miss enough school not to be promoted.

Blessings had helped, I was sure. The year before I was married I asked for a blessing before having my broken back set. I had gone over a cliff on the ski hill and landed in a pine tree. Later, blessings had been imperative before the birth of my five babies. Mel and I even stopped on the way to the hospital with our fourth daughter to have a special laying on of hands for me by my apostle uncle, accustomed to assurance that the power of his office would make the blessing even more effective.

Seventeen years and many blessings after my accident on the ski hill, when I was playing tennis doubles, I'd been hit in the "karate spot" at the back of my neck with a hard serve. I dropped like a rock in a puddle. Men had picked me up and spread me on a narrow bench to carry me up to the clubhouse for help. I felt myself slipping off the bench, but I could not move, speak, or see. We made it to the top just before I would have fallen off. Homer came, took me home to bed, and called a neurologist. My speech and movement came back but not my sight. Tests the next day in the hospital and a devastating headache suggested a blood clot on my brain. Surgery was scheduled.

That night my brothers and Mel gave me a blessing. I was a forty-one-year-old woman with five children at home. During the blessing, I joined in, asking urgently for healing. My headache disappeared. I begged for postponement of the surgery, for a new assessment. Tests the next day showed a clearing of my head. The only residual of the blow was double vision. For two months, I wore a black patch over my right eye to let me see normally.

Not all well-intended blessings were as immediately effective. In the three-and-a-half-year struggle of our daughter Becky's severe bout with manic depression and bulimia, blessings and prayers joined with professional treatment and medication. But in 1970, the stigma of mental illness went hand-in-hand with ancient interpretation. One well-meaning comforter wanted to bless Becky to be rid of the demons that afflicted her. We refused. Never was there a more bleak time for the whole family. Becky did get well, as much because of love as of treatment and faith.

Why wasn't a blessing the first thing I thought of at home in bed after the accident? It never occurred to me to want to bring even that into the vacancy that filled me. Everything in me was on hold.

Only six weeks before, Mel and we who loved him had found comfort in love and the laying on of hands by his bishop and brothers-in-law. Triple bypass surgery was still a major operation, and we were counting on help from the divine. But we had learned since childhood that along with prayers for healing came "Thy will be done" and a hope for peace in the outcome.

Now, the night before the surgery on my face and head, I did ask two brothers, together with Mel, to give me a priesthood blessing. When they put their hands on my head after anointing my forehead with consecrated oil, I remembered how their hands had always before, so many times in my life, been lovingly efficacious. Now those hands felt like a ton of weight on my scalp—as if my neck could not support them—but also as if they were handling the pain. I thought that if they could draw it up in their hands they could pull it off my shoulders, off my whole head, and I would simply float off to where I needed to be, no struggle, no effort at all, just a void of absolute quiet. During the blessing, I silently pled for an escape. I had yet to learn where the accident had taken me.

At 6:20 a.m. the next morning, waiting for surgery, I felt only anticipatory anxiety. I wished desperately for a forbidden drink of water to wash away the taste of blood that continued to coagulate as it ran down my throat from damaged sinuses. "And it will get worse," Dr. Morales said. "You'll bleed through your nose too. Both eyes will be swollen and black."

Lifelong writer that I am, I had taken my journal to the hospital with me. In the bleakness, I spoke to God, barely legibly in my journal, as I often did to my father and mother, by then gone thirty and fourteen years respectively:

> The touch of you has never been absent, only sometimes
> my frail ability to make space for you to come to me. Today
> you are here, gentle fingers on the throbbing in my cheek

and head, telling me that, just as the iron bar of Saturday morning was deflected even as it split the windshield, so the scalpels and whatever else is needed will be guided to give me a new life. I know. And I will honor that life—as I do you this beautiful blue-sky morning. And one more adventure I never could have dreamed of myself.

In my banged-up head, I thought, "On with it now, Lulie. What face you'll come home with, who knows? Who cares really? Everything worth worrying about is totally intact." I had never looked in a mirror.

Dr. Morales did restore me physically. With scrupulous care and skill, and Jim as his assistant, most of the surgery was performed up through my mouth and down through my eye to avoid scarring. The eight fractures in my cheek were anchored by screws to titanium plates around my eye, next to my nose and ear, and under my temple. Only one long cut to close the wound ran from the top of my eyebrow around my eye—barely beyond the socket—into the wrinkles under my eye. A fine reason for wrinkles! In four days, I was home with a message taped to my face: Do NOT MOVE—an edict that might have been laughable in any other phase of my life. Now, with the hospital a memory as dim as time under the anesthetic, pain was my only reminder of anything.

The entry in my journal for Monday, July 7, was a scribble that I could not read back for another seven months:

Awake early with pain, fetid, sore mouth, lips raw, teeth hurting, ears ringing, throat full of blood, wishing I could just start the whole scene over again. All such unreality. Did it really happen? It has to be someone else's experience. It can't keep hurting like this. No plans, no projects, not even any movement. I feel almost intimidated by what has never intimidated me before: sounds, eventualities. I feel weakened and extraneous, like some frail little bird perched in a quivering corner waiting to be carried off on a strong finger to where the sun is shining and songs are being sung. I need to get on my own and be. To quit feeling like a specimen and get on with being a person—whoever that person might be back there in that murky nether realm.

Go back to sleep, Lulie, and find yourself before you wake again. Come on. Sweet sleep—remember? Your friend. Waiting to hold and then spring you like Grandma's arms when you were a little girl.

But it didn't happen.

My family were never far away—Mel, my daughters and sons-in-law, grandchildren, and friends caring about and for me. One friend, a nurse, gave me a back rub every night. Motion of any kind was painful, so my days were spent as a kind of stick figure getting anywhere. I was driven to my writing studio seven minutes away, thinking to recuperate in quiet. Sisters-in-law and dearest friends took turns bringing soup, gruel, or anything that could make it through a straw. I could not have been more lovingly attended nor more graciously offered sustenance for both me and my household. Notes, letters, and tapes to listen to since I could not read; flowers, plants, and food—the offerings of gentle folks familiar and even not—arrived and arrived. I lacked for nothing—and I felt nothing.

For weeks, I did not cry. Neither was I afraid, only trying to understand what happened in that grey region where I was myself but not myself. My journal reflected the struggle:

7:50 a.m. Wed.: . . . maybe just dawning on me what really has happened. And it has happened. Nice cards, visits, great people—but blank.

8:50 a.m. Same: It has to be spirit that is missing. Can't pull up and out. Spoiled by always having the buoyancy pop me off and away no matter what.

My right eye did not like to focus and was extremely sensitive to light even with dark glasses. Any head movement, especially up or down, was painful. I had double vision on both sides. Reading anything smaller than headlines was too much of an ordeal to be inviting. Lowering my head, even to write in my journal, was impossible to bear for more than a few minutes. But feeling nothing was even more foreign to me than lying still and being waited on.

I needed a life, a life impossible now. How to accommodate? April, two months before the accident, had been typically busy with what I loved—our annual girls' trip, my five daughters and I that year together for four days in California; another trip to sunny southern Utah with our family of about twenty, hiking sand dunes and biking in cedar canyons. In the time of my retreat in Sun Valley, I nearly finished a 500-page book about my trip to the Soviet Union in 1984 in the interest of peace. Coming back to Salt Lake, I gave the usual speeches about writing, fitness, believing in God, self, and others. Even though I was atypical as a Mormon woman, spending about as much time away from my home as in it, I spoke to and about women in Mormonism, to church and women's conferences as well as to Rotary Clubs, university classes, and my grandchildren's schools. Just as I loved favorite one-on-one times on birthday sprees with each grandchild, I also relished examining an idea and being invited to explore it with others. Public speaking had become as much my profession as writing or teaching.

Few of my writing friends could understand why time for writing was so hard to find. I was a Mormon woman, often a token woman, but never treated as one. For seventeen years, I was the only woman with general authorities on the board of the church-owned daily *Deseret News*, as well as the first lone woman on the Mountain Bell board. The upheaval of the women's movement was spurring at least tokenism for women in corporate settings. Being reared with brothers,

I knew boy-talk and was not threatened by men in power, nor they by me, in speaking up for women. My sometimes naive, frustrated, and candid questions often opened discussion that was not usual in a bottom-line world. We liked each other.

My family were used to my being away, even as we shared work parties, ski lifts, boating, church, late talks, and cabin time together. In all my busyness, I thrived on mothering. Though often I lived with quiet in my heart, I was swamped by abundance and squeezed into schedules—mostly my own. It was never easy. But would I want to change it? Not likely—surely not because of physical incapacity. I'd find a way, even as I struggled with feeling, as mothers do, that I could never be enough. Surely I'd find a way. The sometimes feeling fragmented, the lack of sleep, the exhilarated exhaustion were worth having that life.

Now, in July, not even able to move my head—how in the world could I manage?

When I had been up and about, I felt like an able and confident part of any family happening. That spring had brought lots to feel anything but glorious about—Shelley and Paul's loss of a newborn baby, Megan's divorce—sad, agonizing for all of us.

Then Mel had his heart surgery, scary, full of urgent prayers. Used to being fit, walking, swimming, he was playing tennis with me when he suddenly couldn't get his breath. Stoic, he at first wanted to wave off any worry, but tests showed he needed immediate surgery. He came home after two weeks in the hospital, thin and depressed, went back to his real estate company too soon, and had a setback. Not uncommon. As with too many, work was his life. Not until our camping trip to Payson Lakes a month later did he venture far from home.

Sunday morning, six days before the accident, Mel was almost well and finally we had a weekend at our cabin in the Wasatch Mountains, twenty minutes from home. I'd lived summers in that canyon since I was born. It was easy to lounge on the deck of the cabin, soaking up the new green of June in the forest around us and reading the 150

Psalms all the way through. Full of cadence, pathos, assurance, and praise, the Psalms had always been some of my favorite scripture. Our Sunday school teacher had asked me to write one to use as an example in his class. Of necessity, my psalm was hasty but something I very much wanted to write—a prayer praising the God of loving-kindness that I had turned to forever. I needed to "make a joyful noise unto the Lord," to say thank you for the healing that had started for Shelley, Paul, Megan, and Mel.

PSALM TO MY CANYON

I awake to the songs of birds;
the sounds of thy creatures awakeneth me.

Thy skies are the blue of thy deepest waters;
deep and broad are they in their invitation
*   to my soul to take flight.*

In mine eyes are thy words;
in my heart the songs of rejoicing in thee.

Blessed, O God, be the quiverings of life
in the branches of trees, in my limbs;
and holy be the sun on the leaves and needles
and on the hair of my head and the feeling beneath it.

I bow to the joy of thy bounty.
I raise up my voice to sing praises
for the grace of thy hand in all the world.

Here in the thickets of thy kindness
and the beauty of thy hand
thou makes me still to know
thou art indeed God.

Six days later came the camping trip to Payson Lakes, fifty miles south of Salt Lake City. It meant Mel's first time out of town after six weeks of recovery. We went with Rinda and Jim's family for a feast—physical, social, and spiritual. Everything delighted: Rinda's mastery of the art of cooking out, Jim's laughing about his fishing, Mel's obvious joy in being among pines and under the sky, and our three grandchildren—full of exploring, games, stories, dirt, and hugs. After a drowsy family prayer, we slept in bags in tents or on the ground under stars, watching our fire go grey and die.

Now this rich kaleidoscope had become bewilderment, surgery, and pain—none of it nearly so hard as the emotional emptiness. Always the question—why? Subsequent journal entries focused often on this question:

Why am I alive when I never should have been? Meg Rampton Munk, a poet friend of friends, forty-three, died today of cancer in Washington DC. Why? And why not me at sixty-two behind a windshield? Every so often crashing in of reality, the smash at the face, the hand up, the eye full of glass, the blood dripping, the disbelief, the mystification—all startling and very down deep terrifying, yet not even frightening in any usual sense, as if I were just part of some pre-scripted drama with no rehearsal and no other performance. And where is the Spirit that has been so present my whole life?

I ended every prayer with, "Please let me just follow my head and breathing into very tired sleep as I always have. And please let my mouth be better." Reacting to heavy antibiotics, I had developed a yeast infection (trench mouth), which complicated the damage to my teeth and gums. Misery there occupied me like some unwelcome tenant filling my brain with dust.

On my ninth day out of the hospital, again I tried to read. Though it felt not too bad, my eye would weep after five minutes or so—

as it did looking down to write a few lines in my journal. I kept telling myself how lucky to have that eye! And my face looking more and more normal as the swelling went down. How easily it might have been scarred or drooping from an injured nerve. Always there were the waves of new awareness of the grace of my being alive, mixed with great washes of black, thinking how grotesquely close I came. And still the bewilderment at being saved. What obligation with that? So far all my senses seemed muted, settled into some blurry region like the print of my pen on the page. I knew I was putting something down, vaguely inside of lines, but I could not read it back, not even the general ideas. Some sharpness, deliciousness had gone.

Was this how other people felt their way through a day? An hour? Without simple pleasures? With my swollen tongue and blistered mouth, food was for ingestion, not tasting, let alone savoring—for sustenance, not delicacy. Would that urgent imbibing return? When? Was this maybe a better way for me to calm these later years—in a gentle nodding state away from the rages and tremors, the ecstasies and flights, leaving them for others to capture?

I felt neutered in every way. My body must have shut down in self-defense. I wanted only to sleep. Was I depressed? Maybe some. But I'd seen clinical depression, the kind that included no hope or relating to the most regular demands of a day. With Becky's three-and-a-half years of recovery from bipolar illness, through a caring doctor and lithium, I'd been in on the terror of departure from reality. This was not that. It was not synapses or chemistry that held me captive. It was the loss of something very precious.

By mid-July I wrote:

I absolutely *have* to get going—get some order back, some pep, some wanting to do anything. Gosh, would I hate to live in the blahs. I feel as if something has to turn up my senses like a gas flame under a teakettle.

But nothing was turning up.

So strange. As though I've died and not gone to heaven but am here seeing what it all would be without me. The cabin, especially so run down in so little time—everywhere inside, dirty, sticky. Outside, dry, my old blue runners sitting on the porch with the brown gloves I used to plant new marigolds by the ramp with Richard the morning of our spree for his eleventh birthday. The cabin smells good—of toast. And all I can think is when will I ever chew again? And no food up here at all for Mel. I've not been to a grocery for over a month. The whole place feels unsupplied, needing a captain *so badly*.

At the funeral for Meg Rampton Munk, a speaker had told of her last question, "Will I ever teach another lesson?" I thought how much I'd loved teaching any and every lesson I'd ever been in on in my whole life—students at the University of Utah, church classes of teenagers, my own daughters in the kitchen, on the tennis court, or ski hill. I wondered if I'd ever teach another anything. At night, I wondered that I ever did any of it at all. I yearned to be outside myself and lost in seeing an idea come alive in dear heads out there somewhere. Nothing is more selfishly demanding than pain. But physical pain can at least be recognized and often dealt with. Emptiness is simply empty. Even Emily Dickinson's hope . . . "the thing with feathers / That perches in the soul," evaded me.

Still, I loved the sun on my face, the face which only weeks before had been bashed by some freaky fluke and then saved by the grace I knew, as I knew the sun would come. Why? How? I felt I would not know until I could say, "Hello!" to another world that I was equally sure of. One Saturday in a burst of faint recognition, I found myself writing in my journal, "Mother and Father, tell me I'm still Lulie, and I'm home, at the cabin."

That night, I had gory nightmares—hatchets in skulls, bodies off balconies. I'd never had bad dreams! The night had been my faithful friend, and the cabin my safest, dearest place. Not wanting to wake

Mel, I left our corner bedroom under the big pine and went downstairs to sit in the old overstuffed chair from the living room of the house I grew up in. I played a tape sent to me by a visionary Catholic friend and listened to Thomas Merton discuss the transcendence of pain. I heard Japanese folk tunes fluted by James Galway. But the dreams kept flashing onto the screen of my mind.

I'd never in my life been a victim of violence. What must it have done to a psyche so preserved in loving-kindness, smashed by a totally chance blow, to come so close to death and yet be saved, to be put back together in essentially the same fashion as before and yet have stretched and screwed and pounded into that same head so much that wasn't there before? How must it be, I wondered, for people who are bludgeoned time after time and by not only chance, but circumstance?

That afternoon, I went to church with my family to welcome a loved twenty-one-year-old nephew back from a two-year Mormon mission. Unfortunately, we sat near the front of the chapel, usually good for seeing. This time seeing became unbearable. After less than half an hour, looking up at the pulpit and into light—even with dark glasses—I had to leave.

In bed at a daughter's home, I felt desolate. I reached into my purse on the night table and pulled out a small notepad I always carried with me. In it I scribbled in a few minutes three singsong verses of loss, not surprisingly resonant of a child's "Now I Lay Me Down to Sleep."

A wizard lived inside my head,
could plan, create and figure.
Never slept except to dream,
my sweet companion wizard.
Calmed me, resurrected me,
gave reason when there was none,
made me believer, celebrator,
Wizard, are you gone?

A genie lived within my heart,
could fathom joys and woes.
Could reach around a thousand souls
and thank with Yes, I knows.
Could yearn, embrace, and kiss and weep,
could soar, take me along.
Genie, I am so alone
without your siren song.

A tiger lived inside my bones,
could muster, leap, and frolic,
take on jungles, find a way,
was seldom melancholic.
Oh forests, where's my tiger hidden?
How deep the dark confoundings?
Without you, Tiger, in my limbs,
pale, wasted are their poundings.

As I finished, a longtime friend and teacher of creative writing at Brigham Young University appeared unexpectedly. I showed her the verses, told her I was blank, that someone else was occupying my skin, that I had not laughed, I had not cried, that I was desperate to feel. I also told her about the hideous dreams. I wanted never to sleep again if I could not ward off their return.

"You'll never have to have dreams like that again," she told me. She had just finished a class on dreams and meditation. She said, "Just watch." She took my hand and started to run her fingers down my arm, bare in the summer heat. "Close your eyes, but pay attention. When I get to the fingers of this hand, you may reenter your dream and change it any way you want. And you'll never have it again."

I lay hoping but not expecting. Her fingers traveled down my arm to my wrist, then to my fingers. Immediately, I was back in my dream, all the fierceness as real as it had been the night before. And I began to change it—like the changes in Kurt Vonnegut's

Slaughterhouse-Five, which I had taught in courses many times. There, Billy Pilgrim, a kind of Christ figure, imagines an end to war like a film running backward. Just as bullets flew back into guns for him and bombs into the bellies of planes—to return to metals in the earth—for me hatchets flew out of skulls, bodies back onto balconies. Blood cleared from wounds and light surrounded me. I sobbed. In that moment, I was happier than I could ever remember being. My friend had come to my rescue. Without ritual, without any usual or obvious access to the sources of well-being, she had demonstrated the power of womanly intuition.

When you move, sometimes it takes time to let your soul catch up to you.

———

With the wizard verses, I knew I was not by any means the same person I had been. I had no notion of what had happened to me in the accident nor of what I scrawled on my journal pages, recording the fluctuations from wondering to accepting, never knowing what to expect. My reaction had never been anger, only puzzlement. I couldn't read back much of it, visually or emotionally, for a long, long time. It was my history, stocked in my journal's attic to someday tell me where I'd been. The night after my experience with dreams, I wrote:

> Maybe the most restorative essence of this time here alone is that for once in my life I don't have to comment. And input is usually audile. I realize how visual it too often is. Now with tapes and inability to look long, especially up or down or sideways at anything, I am being fed in a different region. I'm not trying to remember any more than when I listen to music, just letting it have its way with me, finding its course, settling in. And somewhere, like roots must in rain, the enlivening is beginning, mostly still in the form of

serenity and deep not-having-to. It's as if all the forces in the shape of people in my life are being marshaled somewhere not of my doing and are marching in one by one to rescue me, each with particular gifts or messages, blessing, guiding, reassuring, gathering me home.

I didn't tell Rachel, whom I had met a few months before, about the accident. Back in February, a friend had recommended Rachel to "read my energy." Full of humor, insight, and original metaphors, and young as one of my daughters, Rachel and her gifts were astonishing. Curious about my slow healing, I went to her for another reading. At this point, there were no outward signs of my smashed face.

Yet Rachel said:

You are still you, but pastel, pale and so sad. You are walking very lightly on the earth. You have been to the place of knowing, and you have come back to do something. You have made a promise—to tell us about that place of knowing. Until you can do it, the sadness will be there.

Why should I be sad? I was alive. I was free of the great fear of dying that pursues us. True, I had the displacement of surviving and not understanding why, but she was right. I could remember having forgotten something. I had only the greyness of no desire, the absentness, the loss of wonder. Yet, because I could not read or move freely as I always had, I began to hear some inner music that I had been too busy most of the time to let play. It was all there, waiting to be reconnected. The thought of making those connections did not frighten me. Besides, I began to know what else was there—the other place where beyond my prayers I counsel with my guides, in the time and space where I had made the decision to return.

On my birthday in October, I finished the wizard verse. This stanza jangled less, ending:

My wizard, genie, tiger hold
and whisper This is more.

All parts and passions were healing as my bones and skin had healed. I was beginning to feel a lot, a lot to do with peace.

In January, Rachel asked, "Are you going to have more surgery?" "Not that I know of," I said. In three days, I was in emergency surgery to repair that infected sinus—again, up through my mouth to leave no visible scarring. This time, Dr. Morales also removed an abscess on a nerve to my eye. When I came out of the anesthetic, he held up a page with directions for post-surgery medication and care. Almost afraid to try to look, I opened my eyes. I could focus. Imagine! I could read!

More surgery would be required before I could move fast, put my head down, or look to the side. Six root canals would take away the pain and repair the teeth that had been killed. Still more surgery would free a pinched nerve in my cheek so I could go out in the cold without a face mask. I could be back on a snowmobile to get to the cabin in winter.

Still, getting thoroughly back to myself was a slow, jagged process. Becoming acquainted with what had happened and continued to happen was even slower. It was like a photograph coming out of developing fluid—at first murky, then with an edge here, a detail appearing there, finally the clear view of where I had been.

One morning when I awoke, I knew I had been in that place where I had gone in the accident—my childhood home. It was less of a dream than an awakening to the child life I had known. In my vision, I still knew every castor bean in the spindly garden, every crack in the uneven pavement, where my family—of no age as their forever selves—were waiting for me, a total enveloping of time. Except that today was there too, illuminated softly; the family at the table the way we always sat: Father, Gill, Mother, me, Grandma at the end opposite Father; on the other side, Homer, Richard—three gone, four still here. Then I was almost awake, crying, my tears welling and spilling in a joy beyond joy, everything and everyone utterly dear, accessible, totally there. But I was not separated from now—I was the true me again, in my freedom and rightness—effortless, my being in both worlds.

My journal said I went back and back to it early and late that morning; held, freed, not wanting to leave wherever I was. I could not stop crying—so strange for me, yet that day the only natural thing. I did not want to surface. I could hold to any part of the vision, letting it play back and forth. I was a cloud, formless, in motion but without a road or path, only the sky to float across.

The experience was far beyond ecstasy, joy, or even bliss. And I brought back a word I had intuited should exist—*childness*—not child*like* or child*ish*, but child*ness*. And it was not a dream. I remember the feeling of childness when I see a new baby at a mother's breast or a two-year-old like our final grandchild climbing adroitly into her car seat and saying to her two brothers and the rest of us adults in the van, "Hey guys, I'm happy!" Or in saying a temporary good-bye to a dear one being born into that other world I know to cherish.

After my visit to that other existence, a poem came out of sleep, between sleep and waking. As with the wizard poem, without changing a syllable, I wrote on the pad beside my bed what had been a mystery until that gift from the place of knowing. It was like clearing the windshield for me almost eight months after the accident.

HAVING DIED
OUT OF THE NIGHT: CHILDNESS

More than a state of being
a new being
suffused in light

whatever is there like being held
in Father's arms
way beyond Safe

carried asleep
from one quiet to another

all of it a heartbeat
back back back the coming together
carried in a dark velvet womb
accepting
floating from density
into light

this is only the beginning
whatever that is
I like the others of no age
willing for once to wait
knowing in time
only the exquisite balance
of everywhere at once

saying You are here
come, you of no name
that Emma fits
who hears and answers
the answers

childness knows no blame
only the lightness of being
in your childness
nothing will be lost
though all is right
in the place of no sides at all
of return without going away

Know this that Time is Life
enclave born to other enclaves

As I woke, still scribbling the poem without punctuation, reality began to take hold. The writing was beginning to come from me rather than from some other informing. The poem became mine to explain my return. I realized that this was an interactive process, that I was a participant in what was being given to me by my guides.

> *Every step of the weaning*
> *still heavy on my pillow*
> *the joy is lifted with me.*
> *From even the light am I detached.*
> *It takes me in only*
> *till "love calls me to*
> *the things of this world."*

The line in quotations comes from a Richard Wilbur poem long stored away. With my childness poem, I knew much that I hadn't known before. The poem had made it explicit. Still, it took another friend, Sonia Gernes—poet, former nun, novelist, professor of English at Notre Dame—to speak my change outright. She had been on a Fulbright scholarship in New Zealand and, catching up, I told her of my accident. She was the first ever to actually say what had happened to me. "But of course I understand," she said. "You died."

Later, she sent me an article she had just written about Katherine Anne Porter's *Pale Horse, Pale Rider*. Porter's story, which I had never read, a story most likely autobiographical, was an experience that matched mine in definitive detail:

Moving towards her leisurely as clouds through the shimmering air came a great company of human beings, and Miranda saw in an amazement of joy that they were all the living she had known. Their faces were transfigured, each in its own beauty beyond what she remembered of them, their eyes were clear and untroubled as good weather, and they cast no shadows. They were pure identities and she knew them every one according to their names or remembering what relation she bore them.

She moved among them easily as a wave among waves. The drifting circle widened, separated, and each figure was alone but not solitary; Miranda, alone too, questioning nothing, desiring nothing, in the quietude of her ecstasy stayed where she was, eyes fixed on the overwhelming deep sky where it was morning.

[But Miranda felt] something, somebody, was missing, she had lost something, she had left something valuable in another country, oh, what could it be? There are no trees, no trees here, she said in fright. I have left something unfinished.

Day by day, I was beginning to get used to the idea. I had died. Was death what Rachel meant by "going to the place of knowing"? Was death why I was so profoundly altered? Out of the night, another poem told me:

WAS A WOMAN

Was a woman
a two-part woman
played as if she wasn't
all she was
who passed the middle
of the grave running
into herself trying
to round corners she got
smaller or was it bigger
and had trouble
telling anyone
she had disappeared.

Little by little, I sensed my role, my promise. But how would I talk about it in my conventional spiritual settings? How to tell even my closest family that I had died and yes, gone to a heaven so lovely and full of light and great affection? So different from scriptural descriptions and my learned concepts. So unlike a dream, as real as my mother and father's presence at the table. There never could be any denying of what I now knew had happened. How could I find a believable way to tell about it, much less to explain the grounding I still felt in my traditional faith?

The accident was five years behind me when I attended a meeting of the Utah Women's Forum, where about fifty women of many faiths and areas of expertise gathered. Most of us mothers, we listened to four women in their early thirties tell us about ritual satanic abuse in their childhoods. All four were from different places and backgrounds. Each was now a credible contributor to her own family and work; all told different stories, but chillingly alike.

During the telling, I had a cold shiver from my scalp down the back of my neck and across my shoulders. It never stopped. I knew I was learning about evil, a word I seldom thought about, let alone used. I believed what they were saying. There was no way not to believe—or not to recognize that each needed to be believed in order to get on with her life as a real person, intent on preventing the perpetuation of what had so harmed her.

After the meeting, I talked to each one and told them I believed them and would like more than anything to be able to help. But driving home, I knew there was nothing I could do. I was not in law enforcement, and unlike many at the meeting, I was not a doctor or judge, not a social worker or counselor. I was not even a friend. I tried to tell Mel about what I'd heard, but the facts were too grotesque to repeat. I went to bed thinking I would have dreams as horrifying as the experiences I'd heard about that night. My prayers were for knowing, please, how to help. And, where can I turn for peace?

Not only did I not have bad dreams, but I woke—that is, I roused without opening my eyes—to being suffused in light that held and comforted me. I was immersed in a joy and peace beyond telling. I had revisited that place of knowing. And I knew. I knew that, no, I could not do anything directly for those young women whose stories had so pained me. That would have to be up to others better trained and equipped than I would ever be.

But I could do something. Out of my life of being loved and encouraged, lavished with kindness and understanding, I could try, in telling my stories, to make the light as real and moving as they had made the dark. And hope that I would be believed. Out of the grace offered to me, I could ask for ways to offer it to others. Not only to live with the serenity of abiding in the place of no fear, but to let others know of that place and of the light awaiting them. I had to let them know that such light is available without an iron rod through a windshield. For anyone paying attention and expecting, that grace will open doors to receiving it.

As I had learned to expect, I awoke to another poem:

YOU HEAL

One morning you wake
and everything works
and almost nothing hurts.
After seven months
and the surgery up through
your mouth, screwed to metal plates
you even can focus.

After things happen
you heal. It takes its jagged course
upward and then
believe it or not,
so much for that,
and it is done
the chance of happening.

Then the heart of not
figuring a way back
just happens again
in the still world

like rain running
the skies and green becoming
the hand of the sun.

Eleven years after the accident, another expansion in my understanding of it arose. I was visiting in Oregon for Jim's birthday. On our way to see the movie *Contact*, Rinda, Jim, and I talked about the accident. What had hit me was the L-shaped rod that holds a mud flap on a rig of two or three trailers with up to eighteen wheels. Jim, the scientist, calculated the force of the blow when the three-foot rod flipped up from the freeway and through the windshield—six to eight pounds of iron moving toward us at fourteen miles per hour collided with our windshield moving at sixty-five miles per hour. Several hundred joules of energy, Jim said, dissipated on the end of a rod into my temple. "No way you could have survived, Grey."

But what about my never losing consciousness? How did I ever go to the place of knowing? Why so different than what had been reported over years of tracking and research by both believers and doubters about near-death experiences?

The movie *Contact*, more substantive than usual science fiction, was from a novel by Carl Sagan. In it, Jody Foster's character heads for space in a craft designed by instructions from some far planet. I watched her journey in a state of deja vu: that jolting, confusing, almost violent trip; the special effects simulating "worm holes" through which the spaceship catapults. When she arrives at a shore of infinite beauty where her long-dead father waits with open arms, in astonishment and awe she says, "It's so beautiful. I could never describe this. They should have sent a poet." I held the arms of my seat and couldn't breathe.

When she recounts her journey later, skeptics say impossible, that she was gone only seconds before her craft defaulted. They admit only in private that during that too-brief time, the screen recorded eighteen hours of static. As surely as she knew about her journey and could never deny it, I knew about mine. And I knew I would have to tell about it.

I was crying just as I had in my journal's description of my dying to childness and my return with a promise to keep. On the way home, I sorted my questions again. Had I really never lost consciousness? Jim replayed the blow. "Your head flew back and then forward. Without a seat belt, you would have gone through the windshield. You had to have been knocked out—no way not—and maybe only for a minute."

"And then," he said, "you asked, 'What hit me?'"

I remembered, of course. I told him, "And you said, 'You'll never believe what hit you, Grey.'"

"Yeah. And I still can't," Jim said.

With strange relief, I breathed in a new acquaintance with where I had been. Had I been in on a tesseract described by Madeleine L'Engle decades before in her book that generations of children have loved, *A Wrinkle in Time*? She describes a tesseract:

> . . . a fifth dimension where you can travel through space
> without having to go the long way around . . . or to put it
> into Euclid, or old-fashioned plane geometry, a straight line
> is *not* the shortest distance between two points.

Had I slipped through a "worm hole" by leaving without really leaving? Certainly Einstein had proven this possible. So, here was another clarity to enrich the picture gradually emerging from the murkiness. Without clamor or special effects, in some quiet traveling, I had been to the place of knowing and returned with a view as broad as the galaxies and comforting as my mother's hand. It was obvious again—the pillars of my faith were still intact, but the roof had blown blessedly off the structure to reveal a whole sky full of stars.

CHAPTER 2

PILLARS AND STARS—
TO KNOW AND TELL

Welcome, ancestor. I choose to be a lifetime in your debt. It's a
simple world, full of crossovers. Heaven an airy Somewhere . . .
—Maxine Kumin

Memory is a primary factor in intelligence. Being able to call up that memory can sometimes be anything but easy. What would inch back into my soul and psyche to lend detail and authenticity to what lay behind my injured face and banged-up head? What did I know? To know. Many languages have more than one verb to say "I know." English has only one to express several kinds of knowing.

First, to know with the senses or the mind, a fact: that the iron rod that hit me still stands in a corner of our front closet, three feet tall, rusty, heavy, L-shaped, and that my face is screwed together with titanium plates—facts, provable, real.

Second, the physical: to know how, to be capable of, a capacity. I know how to use this computer or a tennis racquet or the hundred-year-old kettle to make a tasty pot roast dinner.

Third, the social: to know a person, a friend or acquaintance;

further, to enjoy the privilege of deep knowing and being known as I was by my mother and father, as I know my husband, children, and close friends.

Fourth, the emotional: to know what can't be proved or even explained—to know love or fear, believing or skepticism, joy or sadness—private emotional knowing, feelings like those afloat in my wizard verse or in the nightmares at the cabin or in my relief at being able to cry.

Finally, the spiritual: to know spiritual truth, that through knowledge of God, ultimate reality can be obtained through direct subjective experience, as intuition or insight. Until the accident, I knew what I expected of life or an afterlife mostly through my growing up at home and in church. Church, never in the foreground but always in the background of whatever I was about, taught me as my reading and learning from others did. I questioned, searched, believed this, and questioned that. Then came the accident. I was on my own, just my experience to inform me in a whole new way. What would it mean to have the roof blown off the structure of my childhood faith to reveal a whole sky full of stars? Who or what were the pillars? What and where were the stars? I had much to learn. Sometimes that learning comes from simply growing older and coming to know. For me, it evolved from coming to know what my death experience had to teach.

PILLARS

Through her I can look back and remember what is yet to come.

My sense of continuity begins with my early days and my Mormon Church. My two grandmothers, pillars whom I adored, had both been born into polygamous families. My father's mother, Grandma Warner, was born to a sixth wife, and my mother's mother, Grandma

Richards, to a first of four wives.

Among my pioneer forebears, polygamy was not something either to deny or defend. It simply was part of belonging to Mormonism in its early stages—to many members a compelling part, to history a condemning one. As far as I knew, all four of my great-grandparents practiced it as a privilege and duty born of allegiance to their prophets, Joseph Smith and Brigham Young. The practice was a revelation from God. From 1845 until 1890 (when the "Manifesto," a revelation and then a declaration by the prophet, officially ended the practice so that Utah could become a state), worthy members were called to live "the covenant." This was said to be only a small percentage of men holding the priesthood and nearly 50 percent of women at that time. From those happy (for all I knew) alliances came my two grandmothers who swirl in my genes and color my belonging to the family.

In 1859, Grandma Warner was born Minnie Alena Candland. When she was young, her father had packed up their pretty dresses and a few personal treasures, bundled up his wives and their children, and gone from Salt Lake to Sanpete County, on directives of church president Brigham Young. They left a new home with the only papered parlor in Salt Lake City and landed in a dugout with walls that had been mud plastered by bare hands and still bore the fingerprints in the plaster.

At the age of fifteen, Grandma left her home in Mount Pleasant and went to Ogden to take care of her Grandmother Jost, who was ill. There, at eighteen, she met and married William Warner, a tall, good-looking, athletic young man of twenty-two. She had watched him take care of his mother and thought, "A boy who is good to his mother will make a good husband."

They built houses, cultivated farms, moved around Utah—once eight times in one year—had nine children, including my father, their eighth child and youngest son. They moved finally to a farm in Mountain Green because Grandma believed that if they went out on the farm, the children would have the experience they should have. They'd have something to do. They'd be taught industry, get acquainted with soil, get to know livestock, and make finer citizens than if they were raised in the city. But Grandma went to the farm almost by herself, since Grandpa was an engineer on the Union Pacific Railroad and was home maybe one night a week.

She always had somebody living with the family—two girls who didn't have homes and the schoolteacher who boarded with them, besides hired men for the farm work. All of this in a home that had two bedrooms! Her religious life was in service and fun. She loved people and helped everyone she could. She was an organizer and wanted to better herself and other people. She headed bond drives and distributed petitions to get lights and telephones in Mountain Green. She loved rodeos and took her youngest daughter, Edna, on a railroad pass to see them all across Oregon and Idaho.

Saturday was their day for fun. She was organizer and coach of the baseball team. She would roust her boys out early so they could milk the cows and have their chores done. She'd make up a batch of ice cream, take it to the game, sell it with her three daughters, recruit an orchestra, and always have a dance in their barn that night. She even refereed the boys' wrestling matches in the hayloft.

She called on the sick and delivered babies. She was the one to have the first phonograph in the county, one of those with a megaphone and thick round disks. People came from all over to hear it, enjoy her "eats," and have a good time in the big Warner family barn.

Years later, she lived only a few blocks from where my three brothers and I grew up in Salt Lake. She made the most tender buttermilk biscuits and the most tangy lemon meringue pies for our ward dinners. She must have been in church, but I never knew it. She died at seventy-eight of diabetes, when I was ten. Because she figured little in my daily life, her death seemed distant. I only remember her in her coffin in their living room and barely remember her funeral in our Highland Park Ward.

Grandma Emma Louise Stayner Richards lived with us. Born in 1856, she was only sixteen when her mother died at forty-one.

Family legend had it that her mother, Emma Turner Stayner, died of a broken heart when, over the years, her beloved Arthur took three other wives. Grandma, the eldest of seven, was left to help her well-educated and somewhat frail father, Arthur Stayner, rear the family. At seventeen, Grandma Richards ignored public opinion and became one of three women to enter the first class of the University of Deseret in Salt Lake City. It was said that she had the ability to read a book in an hour and report on its contents in a way that made it more interesting than the original. Her love of literature, mathematics, and history influenced her future family more than any formal schooling they would ever receive.

When she was nineteen, she met and married Stephen L. Richards, son of Dr. Willard Richards, who had been one of three men with the prophet Joseph Smith when Joseph was murdered in Carthage Jail in Missouri. Stephen also came from a polygamous family, the son of his father's fifth wife of twelve. Stephen worked on the railroad to support his widowed mother but harbored a longing to be a doctor like his father. It took six years of encouragement from Louise, together with sixteen-hour days laying railroad ties, for them to save enough to realize his dream of going to medical school.

Because there was no medical school in Salt Lake City, this meant leaving his wife and small children for nine months every year, coming home to work summers to scrape together enough to send him off again in the fall. During those five years, Louise had a total of six children and no real income. One year she lived on thirty-five dollars, cultivated a garden, befriended Indians, and earned a reputation for being the best cook in the county.

Often she sewed late into the night making over the hand-me-downs of one brother for another. Her six boys never wore a "store-bought" suit until they started at the university. By the time her husband was able to set up his medical practice, nine of their ten children were born and Louise took over as his practical nurse in their home. She administered anesthetics, calmed frightened patients, washed bedclothes, and sterilized instruments. My mother told me that her father was so meticulous that in forty years of practice, he never lost a mother in childbirth—a remarkable record for the turn of the century.

Into the roomy, gracious Salt Lake home of the Richards family on Ninth East by Parley's Creek came not only children and patients but crowds of children's friends—to ride ponies, pull taffy, and sing in the parlor. My mother, the youngest in the family, grew up reading and drawing; she was the pet of her six older brothers and much older sister, whom she worshiped. Despite the sorrow and loss of two children in early childhood—and later the death of that older daughter, Alice, just two weeks before her marriage—the Richards family knew gaiety and warmth, due mostly to the humor, patience, and expansive affection of their mother.

Into their lives she also brought the richness of service, both at home and in the church, where she served among other things for ten years as Relief Society president. When asked how she had such good luck in rearing her family, my grandma usually answered, "It wasn't luck. I stayed home and I told them stories." Much as my mother did with us.

Grandma Richards had been a widow since before I was born. She belonged to literary groups and produced countless afghans, needlepoint chair covers, and much anticipated surprises for all of us for our birthdays and Christmas. She called me her little shadow, and when I was small, she let me sleep in bed with her. She was a presence.

In our home, my grandma's six devoted sons, two of them being general authorities of the Mormon Church, visited her at least once a week in her upstairs living room in our house for humorous or serious counsel. They amused us and brought treats, cures, and magic tricks with their hearty visits. With equal zest, she welcomed her one son who came from out of town and smoked, as we scurried to find our one ashtray, entranced by our exotic uncle. She was a queen in our home, for her wit and wisdom as much as for her sturdy, regal cheerfulness.

I never remember seeing this grandma in church either. Yet her sense of God and his constant availability peppered every conversation I can remember with her. In her later years, she traveled extensively and was seldom home. But her death when I was twelve stayed with me. My first encounter with wondering about a hereafter was written forty years later:

FIRST LOSS

My grandma shared her bed with me.
We slept with breaths that matched.
(I went to sleep every night restraining
deliberately one extra breath in five
to let her slower time teach mine to wait.)

She never knew I waited, but talked
to me of Mendon where Indians searched
her isolated young-wife home for cheese and honey,
and of Santa Barbara and eerie tides that
drew her now for gentle months away from snow,
and sometimes of Evangeline lost in the forest primeval.

Grandma's batter-beating, white-gloved, laughing
daytime self slept somewhere else, and she visited
mellifluous beyond my ardent reach, always off
before me. I followed into rhythms I knew
were good, her chamois softness weighing me
by morning toward a cozy common center.

She died there when I was twelve.
I was sleeping, alien, down the hall
in a harder bed, isolated from the cancer
that took its year to take her.
That night my mother barely touched my hair

and in stiff, safe mechanics twirled the customary
corners of my pillow one by one. "Grandma's gone,"
she said. Crepuscular against the only light
alive behind her in the hall, she somehow left.
My covers fell like lonely lead on only me.
I lay as if in children's banks of white where
after new snow we plopped to stretch and carve

our shapes like paper dolls along a fold.
Now, lying on my back, I ran my longest arms
from hip to head, slow arcs on icy sheets,
and whispered my childhood's chant to the breathless room:
"Angel, angel, snowy angel, spread your wings and fly."

I suppose, looking back at my grandmothers' lives, the thing I remember most about each of them is a feeling of their being real, of knowing who they were, what they stood for, of trusting that, of feeling trusted by them. Beyond even this trust, I realize now, was a "proverbial" sense of joy and expectation. Those grandmothers, and my parents, lived by a practical application of Proverbs: "A merry heart doeth good like a medicine: but a broken spirit drieth the bones." Ours was that kind of religion.

At the same time, in our household of love, faith, and good humor, we never talked about some very *real* things. Grown-ups dealt in private with any dissention or disaster in our extended families, keeping big problems away from little ears. I long now to visit with those dear progenitors about their lives beyond the kitchen or living room—and especially about the church. What did they believe and feel? What did they know and then choose to keep to themselves? We simply absorbed by some spiritual and very effective osmosis the certainty of being contributors and lifetime members of the church, of marriage in the temple for time and all eternity, and raising the families that we surely would have, to do the same.

Still, it had to be my pillars—those grounded, solid, joyful folks—who continue to help me bridge my Mormon faith and my connection to all kinds of other believers or nonbelievers as well as to ideas and stars. From my two grandmothers, through my mother and father, I inherited my hybrid self—the girl who rode horses and played ball; the girl who played with dolls, read, and ruminated. Starting as early as seven, I belonged to two worlds:

SUNDAY SCHOOL PICTURE

Our Ward housed
the biggest Sunday school the church has ever let exist.
One Sunday morning a thousand of us
hipped into the breathless benches
and undulated into the foyer, ante room
recreation hall,
and up onto the indignant stage
a thousand Mormon heads away from the pulpit.

In the picture
that President Heber J. Grant had them take
that auspicious day (three shots overlapping)
I came out twice, being on the edge of two of them,
and Mother always said that would guarantee me
two chances at perfection, but I being seven at the time,
*   figured, so?*
and went on becoming
two people instead.

The poem goes on about me, the adventuresome girl, slipping through a window into the empty church with her brothers to play "The Happy Farmer" on the cool, black pedals of the organ and, with rapid eyes, to see what other kinds of bathrooms looked like. Then about me, the ladylike little girl in Sunday school with tortuous ringlets and buttoned velvet, hoping that the deacons were noticing that I could read the words to "I Know That My Redeemer Lives" and that I swallowed the sacrament water slowly and tried to think of Jesus all white as in the grove, not with his beard crumpled on his collarbone, dead.

> *Sometimes I look*
> *at that thousand-peopled picture when I'm sorting*
> *things and marvel a lot, and even otherwise, I find*
> *myself saying, Highland Park Ward, my roller skates*
> *still rattle down your dented driveway, and*
> *my absent waiting is sometimes done against*
> *the brown banisters below the huge painting of the pioneers*
> *and their covered wagons*
> *over the door beyond your raised entry,*
>
> *and mostly, your organ*
> *churns under its outside loft across the filled fields*
> *where our shortcuts are long buried in old foundations,*
>
> *and like the green-grained oak*
> *of your chapel doors, it closes with gentle right*
> *my separateness and gathers my wandering*
> *double selves together.*

Through the accident I learned a harmony I had sought all my life, realizing my hybrid self fit anywhere. In my death experience, I was one person—an eternal essence, whole, loved, beyond expectations of a culture or even a family. In my childness, I simply *was*.

Church in my growing-up years had much less structure and stricture than it does now. We four children regularly attended Sunday school on Sunday morning, but almost never the sacrament meeting at the ward in the evening. Being at every meeting at the ward for about three hundred families in adjacent blocks was not the measure of being a faithful Mormon. Nor can I remember my parents reading scriptures, though my grandmother gave me her tattered New Testament. That, I read in private in my teenage years as I kept my diaries every night at Mother's old pull-down desk in my room. The family spent Sundays visiting, taking rides, having dinner and naps, playing Ping-Pong in the basement, throwing balls, sledding in the street, or listening to Charlie McCarthy or President Roosevelt on the radio by the fire. On Sundays, Father met with the athletic committee of the general board for the youth of the church, where he was instrumental in initiating a worldwide basketball program for young men. We paid by far more attention to the finals of those games in the Deseret Gym than ever to semiannual general conference in the Tabernacle on Temple Square.

With the same *joie de vivre* and imagination that Mother brought to our building bookcases and making scrapbooks, she taught nine-year-old boys in Primary on Tuesday afternoons. She ended their year with a marble tournament and prizes of her hand-stitched knuckle savers for playing on hard dirt (one for me too). That teaching job was Mother's only church activity, except for coming to meetings when any of us or her grandchildren were performing. But her faith and prayers guided our days and nights like a beacon in the dark. Our most churchy times were in the summer on Sundays at the cabin.

It was Grandma Richards's cabin, built before the turn of the century in a Wasatch Mountain canyon just beyond Salt Lake. We were there almost the day school was out for the summer and stayed until it started in fall. With my brothers and eight cousins near my age to explore with, I was in heaven.

Like Grandma Warner did as a young wife, Grandma Richards had a Victrola. We'd wind its handle—I still can hear out of the megaphone, its one-sided, thick, scratchy recording of Caruso or a hymn we loved, "Our mountain home so dear, / Where crystal waters clear / Flow ever free." And from the breathy pumpings of her ancient organ spilled out, "For the strength of the hills we bless thee, / Our God, our fathers' God." Or "Danny Boy" that I learned at ten to play for my father. On a screened porch under giant pines, sometimes sixty relatives living in the canyon, in clean starched shirts with our canyon pants tucked into our boots, sang together. "The spirit of God like a fire is burning . . . / We'll sing and we'll shout . . . / Let glory to them in the highest be given." And, oh we gave it—the glory—and receive it still from those mountains. And from those dear rugged and refined people, lasting as the landscape we all belonged to, "Henceforth and forever, Amen and Amen."

Right after our half hour of school time—arithmetic, spelling, and reading—most richness came as it would to a creature of the earth turned unbelievably loose by our otherwise knowing mother. To be part of the canyon was as simple as making moss villages on the islands in the flat stretch of stream, digging a hole for hiding underground, shinnying the powder-white trunk of an aspen, riding bareback on my uncle's pony, killing rattlesnakes as taught by Mother, or climbing with Father to the giant rock armchair on the highest ridge to look for forty miles in any direction—all of it and us shimmering in ninety-five dry degrees in July.

I slept with Grandma at the cabin too, where she talked to me of fairies and told of Pegasus, the flying horse. Every night, I would ride away on him above the high clump of maples into the starry sky beyond Crow's Nest Mountain. I belonged in the vastness with the Heavenly Father we prayed to, as loving and as real as my grandmother's hand on my shoulder.

On a slant of sheltered shingled roof still hanging over the added-on room where Grandma and I slept, I made a playhouse. I'd hoist my bottom over a two-by-four rafter and play there with my dolls, stories, and kittens, deliciously alone and feeling close to Bible-story people—Daniel and David, Ruth and Mary—whom I knew like my own aunts and uncles. When it rained, I'd listen to the rattle on the shingles and watch for the lightning over the mist against the mountains, waiting in sumptuous awe for the thunder, far more excited than frightened. Half a century later, I would write about being out in the storm with my cousins:

NIGHT THUNDER AT THE CABIN

In thunder at 2 a.m.
I occupy all my lives
my loves hovering holding
rising with me to the wild night
real as photos I tacked in daylight
to the rough wood wall above the stairs
or secret in the wardrobe of my mind.

Electric, shuddering in wanting more,
the lightning out of sight,
in memory I make my own.

Effortless, taken dripping wet
I mount the sapling maples
where, still small, my brothers and six cousins fled
to fly in windy thunder storms,
my ringlets sloshed to curly curl,
my arms and legs wrapped around a slim trunk
like binding on a sprain
till ecstasy let one hand loose
to open to the raging sky
a cup of fingers
reaching for the rain.

From that sturdy brew of the earthy and the eternal, the spirited and the spiritual, I am still sent forth "with joy, and . . . led forth with peace: the mountains and the hills shall break forth before you into singing, and all the trees of the field clap their hands" (Isaiah 55:12).

At home or in the canyon, it was that mix of life and church—never static, never separate, and seldom somber. Meetings? None except for Sunday school, attended not at all regularly. More often we met on Sundays at 7:00 p.m., the family having sandwiches made by me of leftover roast by the fire until dating times. Testimony? To the goodness of God, of life, people, and engagement with both. Church? Mostly acknowledged by not smoking or drinking, adhering to the Word of Wisdom and a way of life that allowed everything else to be more alive. Joseph Smith? Many years into my adulthood, when asked by a Jewish poet friend why I stay in my Mormonism, I explained it with a story, the details recounted by my mother. It is my mother's story transposed into an allegory about my believing.

When I was a little girl, my father took me to hear Helen Keller in the Tabernacle. I must have been about eight or nine and I'd read about Helen Keller in school, and my mother had told me her story. I remember sitting in the balcony at the back of that huge domed building that was supposed to have the best acoustics in the world. Helen—everybody called her that—walked in from behind a curtain under the choir seats with her teacher, Annie Sullivan. Helen spoke at the pulpit—without a microphone—but we could hear perfectly, her guttural, slow, heavily pronounced speech. She spoke about her life and her beliefs. Her eyes were closed and when it came time for questions from the audience, she put her fingers on her teacher's lips and then repeated for us what the question had been. She answered questions about being deaf and blind and learning to read and to type and, of course, to talk. Hearing that voice making words was like hearing words for the first time, as if language had only come into being—into my being at least—that moment.

Someone asked her, "Do you feel colors?"

I'll never forget her answer, the exact sound of it—"Some-times . . . I feel . . . blue." Her voice went up slightly at the end, which meant she was smiling. The audience didn't know whether to laugh or cry. After quite a lot of questions, she said, "I would . . . like to ask . . . a fa-vor of you." Of course, the audience was all alert. "Is your Mormon prophet here?" she asked. There was a flurry of getting up from the front row, and President Grant walked up the stairs to the stand. She reached out her hand and he took it. All I could think was, "Oh, I wish I were taking pictures of that."

"I . . . would like . . . ," she said, "to hear your organ . . . play . . . your fa-mous song—about your pio-neers. I . . . would like . . . to re-mem-ber hear-ing it here." All the time she was speaking she was holding his hand he had given her to shake. I liked them together, very much.

I remember thinking, "I am only a little girl (probably others know) but how in the world will she hear the organ?" But she turned toward President Grant and he motioned to Alexander Schreiner, the Tabernacle organist who was sitting near the loft. At the same time, President Grant led her up a few steps to the back of the enormous organ—with its five manuals and eight thousand pipes. We were all spellbound. He placed her hand on the grained oak of the console, and she stood all alone facing us in her long, black velvet dress with her right arm extended, leaning slightly forward and touching the organ, with her head bowed.

Brother Schreiner played "Come, Come, Ye Saints," each verse a different arrangement, the organ pealing and throbbing—the bass pedals like foghorns—as only he could make happen. Helen Keller stood there—hearing through her hand and sobbing.

Probably a lot more than just me—probably lots of us in the audience were mouthing the words to ourselves—"Gird up your loins; fresh courage take. / Our God will never us forsake; / And soon we'll have this tale to tell— / All is well! / All is well!" I could see my great-grandparents, converts from England, Wales, France, and Denmark, in that circle of their covered wagons, singing over their fires in the cold nights crossing the plains. Three of them had babies die; my great-grandmother was buried in Wyoming. "And should we die before our journey's through, / Happy day! / All is well! / We then are free from toil and sorrow, too; / With the just we shall dwell! / But if our lives are spared again / To see the Saints their rest obtain, / Oh, how we'll make this chorus swell— / All is well! / All is well!"

So then—that tabernacle, that singing, my ancestors welling in me, my father beside me, that magnificent woman, all combined with the organ and the man who played it and the man who had led her to it—whatever passed between the organ and her passed on to me.

I believed. I believed it all—the seeing without seeing, the hearing without hearing, the going by feel toward something holy, something that could make her cry, something that could move me, alter me, something as unexplainable as a vision or a mystic connection, something entering the pulse of a little girl, something that no matter what would never go away. What it had to do with Joseph Smith or his vision or his gospel I never would really understand—all I know to this day is that I believe.

With that mystic connection, I believe in it. I get impatient with people's interpretations of it, with dogma and dictum, but somewhere deep inside me and far beyond impatience or indifference there is that insistent, confounding, so help me, sacred singing—"All is well! / All is well!" My own church, inhabited by my own people. With my own feel for its doctrines, it is my lamp, my song—my church. I would be cosmically orphaned without it.

Beyond that, a believing too in an afterlife and the divinity of Jesus Christ came as certain as daybreak.

If Mother and Father talked about scripture, it was to make a point, talking much more of the "blessed are theys" and the "thou shalts" than the "thou shalt nots." In Grandma's New Testament gift to me, I read the Beatitudes in the way I kept my diaries—at my desk in my room and in private, the whole orientation always more private than proclaimed.

The priesthood of my father or uncles was like the dew from heaven distilling power to heal my combination measles and whooping cough when I was four—blessings ever since full of assurance and cure. It was the gentle authority of my father making sure with the bishop that I, a year younger than my school friends, be promoted with them and not held back by instructions from authorities that demanded otherwise. I never questioned until I was a grown woman the rights of my brothers in church ordinances.

From Mother came the faith, constant. Prayer? As certain of efficacy as the predictions of the barometer that came across the plains in a covered wagon with my pioneer great-grandfather and was never wrong. Though sometimes filled with the clichés of overused phrases, Mormon prayers are intended to be spontaneous entreaties and expressions of gratitude. While speaking in public has become natural for me, praying in public never has. To me, prayer is too private, too personal, too much a part of my most intimate being to be made public. Any formal prayers that I've given I have written first to stay in the realm of outward expression.

Love? Never even wondered about. A loving Father in heaven—simply an extension of a loving father at home. Our family may sound like the pabulum sweetness of TV's *The Waltons*, but our growing up was thoroughly real. My brothers wrestled constantly—my mother would say "tussled"—and sometimes got hurt, but being a girl with no sister to compete with, I was their cheerleader, never sorry that they were my brothers. Often I was irritated at not being allowed their privileges, from going with Father to learn to swim, naked, at the Deseret Gym to being the one to call on the phone for a date. As a four-year-old, I cried to go with the boys and Father to sit with the players at a game he was refereeing, saying, according to Mother, "Here I am four years old and I've never seen a football game!"

Father furnished the athletic, Mother the aesthetic; he the extroversion, she the contemplative; both of them with humor and love of people, both with expectation that we would use our heads and our hearts in following any bliss.

I felt part of a heritage of pioneers and pluck, with anything possible, the grace of God visible in every tree, bird, and excitement of body or mind. But even so, for me there was always wondering. Not doubting—*wondering* about institutionalizing belief. Why?

One Sunday night, my three brothers, their wives, and my husband and I sat around the old, black Monarch stove at our cabin and talked, as we had at someone's home on the first Sunday night of every month for nearly forty years, on "Fast Sunday" when our offerings from a twenty-four-hour fast would be contributed to the welfare plan for those in need. We talked about growing up in the church. We remembered. We listened. We laughed a lot. We knew more than we had before.

But even in this group of my dears who have been in on much of my growing up in the church, there were interpretations of church orientation as various as our feelings were harmonious. My brothers had married bright, talented, loving women who had grown up in much more church structuring than we had in our casual taking on of Sunday and its meetings, let alone the study of scriptures and exact marking of every church roll. My brothers had all been bishops (as had Mel) yet no two of us siblings remembered things exactly alike; at the same time, each of us remembered our ease and joy in growing up Mormon in a day when structure and stricture played such smaller roles.

How did I get to be one who sees all sides of a question? To be full of faith even as I'm full of questions? One who sees a lot more grey than either white or black? And yet be one of the privileged partakers of the simplest answer to growing up at all—in or out of anything—love. I have been offered it at every turn: at home, in the church, in the neighborhood, on committees, and in classrooms. I know and feel for the enormous responsibility of the men and women who are called to make worldwide decisions and who live with scrutiny that would beleaguer a microbe under a microscope. I have been longtime friends with many of the general authorities as well as public officials and know that, like my husband and brothers and their wives, they are men and women who are human even as they are basically of good will. I know and respect too some of those most intent on that kind of scrutiny. What else but to grieve when the two do battle and make headlines? When divisiveness cuts into the heart of my community?

In my growing up, loyalty and trust, the basic elements in any relationship, came with affection and rooting and crying for each other. But by the time I was a college girl, I wanted independence desperately, to have a summer job—away, like my friends. Father wanted me home to help Mother, saying I never would want for anything. Money I never did want for, but freedom I did. Mother, an artistic, meticulous little lady, always had help at home—a live-in girl till I was twelve. Then I became an often resentful cook and keeper of the house.

Though of course I dated, played tennis, rode horses, and had access to the cabin, I could feel very sorry for myself as my friends went off to Zion or Yellowstone summer adventures and my brothers went to work in a logging camp or to drive cars from Detroit for my father's business. Whether they were gone or home, I picked up their rooms, made their beds, ironed their starched shirts and tennis shorts, put on their meals, saw them off to priesthood meeting before Sunday school, and always expected the question, "Who will help Emma Lou with the dishes?" None of it was a matter of priesthood authority or Mother's compelling, but simply the way things had been done in a family rooted in tradition. Besides, I just plain loved them, and praise from the boys and Father never was unimportant.

Rebellion? Against the housework sometimes, but not against what I loved: the sun coming up over Pine Top Mountain. Snow curtaining against the streetlight. Father happily stomping his day off on the back porch—home from a sales trip, a meeting, refereeing a football game. Mother setting up her easel, the smell of oils and turpentine. Hitting balls or skiing with my brothers. Time in a room of my own to imagine and dream, read and write, say my very private prayers, mostly, "Help me to be a good girl and help me to deserve." Often a close friend to invite to the cabin in place of the sister I never had.

God? Easy to believe in, like a divine extension of Father and Mother on the sidelines at our tennis matches. Usually, the finals were on Sunday, right after Sunday school, the only time we played on Sunday. If we weren't playing, we were in the bleachers at old Forest Dale rooting, in the then-decorous tournament silence of a tennis match, for someone else in the family. Father's motto—"Try hard, play fair, have fun"—easy words to translate into a divine will that we never talked about but understood. He knew we knew the rules and how to play the game, and we were on our own on the court—no saving us from our own dumb or tense mistakes. In the bleachers, Father could only watch and root, not coach, keeping a list of errors and placements that we could look at later if we chose; Mother never missing a point in the game. As we came off the court, there they were, smiling; both with their arms open to console or celebrate. They let each of us know we had done all right. More important, that we were loved.

My early morning seminary teachers at East High gave me my first exposure to theology in the Bible and the Book of Mormon, and my institute of religion classes at the university offered sustenance to my fragmentary gospel knowledge. But everywhere there were teachers—at home, church, and school—tennis and college friends of every faith teaching me about mercy and justice and goodwill. Always mentors of good sense and restraint guided me, with as much humor as solemnity, on committees and boards, in classrooms and study groups. Especially in poetry, from Pulitzer winners to friends at artist retreats, willing and gifted teachers of a dozen faiths continue to inspire and coach me in much more than the language of poetry.

As always, now at eighty-six, I maintain my touch with my mountain home. In June, I declare a "sabbatical" from city life and obligations. I tell my bishop I'll be back to church in September. I get to be that woods creature again. Family and friends come to enrich my green world and it them. With my pillars alive in my being, hymns and operas accompany prayers as I play out my childness in God's presence.

Each of us must find our own abiding. Obviously, ancestral layering—the combining of family history and natural beauty—play a big part of my spiritual grounding. But not everyone need have a family cabin or pioneer ancestors to find solace and congruity in a personal setting. When I come to the cabin, I step out of my normal life, take time to pay attention to trees and sky, stop the rush and routine of my crowded days. For many, such a stepping out can be to the ocean or the prairie or a room of one's own. My friend and editor finds spiritual space on an island in the San Juans; my brother found it on his sailboat. My husband and one daughter find it swimming; others in running or gardening; some sitting in the sun, others in the shade. Many find it in a cathedral or yoga session or in the celestial room of the temple. It is an honoring of self that demands such departure from the usual—to leave open spaces for spirit to enter.

February 20, 1956, Father died at fifty-nine of a stroke when I was in the hospital under an oxygen tent with pneumonia. I was thirty-one. My doctor brother and Mel came to my room to tell me. He was just a floor below me, brought from his office by an ambulance. He had called me that morning to say, "I've got a surprise for you, Sweetie—a new mattress to replace the one from the Deseret Industries you and Mel have been sleeping on for all these years." I never got to say good-bye. I went to his funeral at my old Highland Park Ward, heard his friends tell of his humanity, strength, and love. I was rushed back to bed and could not go to his burial. For months, even years, I woke in the night as if interrupted in the middle of a conversation, thinking of what I wished we could have talked about. Death was a specter. No "Angel, angel, spread your wings and fly." Though I believed still in that angel life, the reality of my loss was overwhelming.

Six months later came another death, a friend far too young to die. Devastation. That morning in September goes slamming off without me. "She died fifteen minutes ago." No! So alive. Sick only forty-eight hours. Diane, only twenty-eight years old, at 6:44 a.m.

The voice from the polio ward at the County Hospital. "Are you family?"

"No, just a friend."

Just a friend. My friend so close I pick up the phone after her funeral and dial her number. That day my husband and our three daughters under five sleep a Sunday-morning sleep, the house for me is suddenly a suffocation. In my stupor, I am in the car driving my way, my only way, to my comfort, my mountains holding up the pale sky.

On the road behind my empty eyes, my friend rises to meet them, my mountains. Our ten years of being in on each other's lives melt into this one Sunday morning. My canyon opens around me, its arms hold me. My blonde, blue-eyed friend and I are again playing tennis, introducing each other to the boys we will marry, confiding the coming of babies, singing in sacrament meeting, "In Our Lovely Deseret," skiing the hills and lakes, teaching at the same school, laughing, laughing, laughing.

Maples, birches, pines, and kinnikinnick reach for each other, for me, in a tunnel of green; the slim brown road sings its dirge under my tires. I hear her sextet singing, "In the same way then, but I can't remember where or when." The sky becomes the purple blue of sadness. Her small children bewilder before me, two struggling on short understandings to find her, the baby unyielding in others' arms, their father disappearing into his disbelief. How ever to let their loss, mine, fade into these trees of my childhood? "Maybe with snow," I think, "surely the snow just weeks away will level the pain, give silence to the creek that will weep under its ice and send all creatures to frosty sleep. Remember," I tell myself, "how inevitable the passing death of the seasons. How alive under each winter are the thousand colors of green waiting."

But I know this is only the beginning of the dying. How will I fathom the others to come? The disappearance of who is there? What do I know of death and its claiming those I love? Into the grassy-centered drive, across the wooden bridge, at the foot of great hovering Castle Crags, the car stops at the path to the brown cabin. The whole canyon is alive with tremblings and songs. In some familiar distance I hear what I learned in seventh grade chorus, "Goin'

Home"—"Mother's there, 'spectin' me, / Father's waitin' too; / Lots o' folk gather'd there, / All the friends I knew." And they're not even gone yet.

I look up through the trees to the now hazy sky. Where are you, my friend? Why this ending? I am thirty-one and naive as when Grandma died when I was twelve. As uninformed and soul-lonely as when Father died only months ago. "Lullaby and good night . . . "— what I sang to comfort my babies. The years tug at my face, tears scald inside with not letting go. Up through the tops of trees the vastness moans to me, "Cry—cry please"—the balm of tears. The great gap of her being gone consumes me.

I am sobbing. Some deep mending has begun. In my canyon and beyond, in that moment I think I know something—but what? More, even than the solid believing of my pillars and my upbringing, offers confirmation and lasting solace.

I would say good-bye to many friends, bring my understanding to many funerals, but the greatest commemoration of my friend was yet to come. Born the following year, our fourth baby, sent I was sure by divine grace and her namesake. Blonde and blue-eyed among dark-haired sisters, we would name her Diane—but because I hadn't the heart to call her that, we nicknamed her "Dinny."

It would not be until double my age then, at sixty-two, with a shaft of iron through the windshield, that I would know what I longed to know in the deaths of Father and Diane.

That knowing was hinted in the death of my mother. For fifteen of the sixteen years before her death, Mother lived with us in a wing of her own in the house she, Mel, and I built together two years after Father died. As Grandma Richards had been for me, Mother was resident matriarch for our five daughters. But unlike Grandma, since Mother was almost always home, she could be both inspiration and irritant as she brought her fastidious notions of growing up to their teenage music, short skirts, and ever-present boyfriends. Solid Mel was her best friend and I, with my comings and goings, her challenge.

Teaching part-time English at the university and serving on community and church boards, being tennis coach, writer, and friends with those like and unlike me, I loved mothering most of all—but not all the time. For Mother, whose entire life had been spent at home or with her Friday sewing club or Thursday literary group, my complex doings looked sometimes like neglect of what she deemed most important. In many ways it was. It was also my lifeline. I often felt resentful, if not repentant, because of her wishing I were different.

Just before Thanksgiving in 1972, she had a massive heart attack. Three weeks later, we brought her home, knowing that she would never want to die in a hospital. She kept her sense of humor and appreciation, as well as her dignity, as I got to read our old poems to her and bathe her as I had my babies. My brothers and their wives helped, came to visit, and laughed, making crazy toasts with 7-Up in bud vases. Our daughters played music on their violins, piano, and flute she'd put up with in their not-quite-beautiful beginnings. We all had family prayers for peaceful exiting of her full-of-grace life. My brothers took turns sleeping on a cot beside her bed at night so she would never be alone. Close as we became, she and I talked about everything but death.

Then, by her bed on her last day, I held her hand and she clung to mine. She spoke inaudibly for hours to someone, not me. I could feel an inner battle going on as she, the last leaf on her family tree, talked to those she loved beyond the veil as she still yearned to be with us, her family holding onto her here. I was part of the indescribable passing from one state of being to another. How to let her go? Through her lifetime of "working on the weather," praying us through crises, showing us how to give—goods, time, interest, ourselves—demonstrating a caring, laughing, loving, expectant way to go, Mother had managed it all. She had preserved believing and had led us quietly, inconspicuously, in the paths of righteousness—and even mischief. She had made those paths flower with fun, good spirit, and camaraderie along with deserved criticism. Whatever storms there had been—and there were many—had been met with the certainty that they would pass, and that like Job, where we could not control our circumstances, we could control our responses.

And now I was losing her, Grace, my pillar. I leaned close to her, concerned that she hear, as she always had, my concern. I'd been a daughter different by far than the one I'd always imagined her wanting—a needlepoint, demure daughter more like her than my athletic, involved father. We'd joked about it before, but now I said, "Mother, I know you've always wished I'd taken a gentler horse."

She opened her brown eyes, flashing in dark-circled settings, squeezed my hand harder, and said, "No. I've always loved you on the wild one."

That night just before Christmas, I had to let her go. While smiling at some violets that had just arrived, Mother gasped and was gone. Alert and wise to the end, she remained my link with how to do it. Traditional as she was, and private, compelled by her own understated faith, I know she would hear my coming-to-know story and revere it. She believed in fairies on the roof and the Holy Ghost alive in our hearts. Beyond that, she also believed in me. That I died and came back with a promise that would involve a lot more than a ride on the wild horse might not even surprise, let alone scare her.

With the pillars of my faith still intact, what difference did my accident make to my knowing? Now it was the telling that I had to let go of.

STARS

Celestial objects / the farthest are the earliest / the oldest the brightest . . .

—May Swenson

After my accident, my believing took on a new dimension. My childhood faith could remain intact even as I learned about a different place of knowing.

Those seven months when I couldn't read allowed me a new kind of seeing and hearing, not unlike the cataract surgery later that cleared black goo from behind my aging irises or the new eardrum built by a specialist to restore hearing in my ear devastated by an infection. Much earlier with all my faculties intact, the likes of E. E. Cummings had appealed to me with his "i thank You God for most this amazing / day . . . (now the ears of my ears awake and / now the eyes of my eyes are opened)."

And Rumi, my favorite mystic poet:

> The big ear on the outside of our head should be closed.
> It is so good at hearing that the inner ear goes deaf. . . .
> Our sounds, our work, our renown, these are outer.
> When we move inwardly, we move through secret space.
> Our feet walk firmly, they experience sidewalks well.
> There is one inside who walks like Jesus on the sea.

Or my mentor William Stafford, "In the All-Verbs Navaho World":

> Change your live-here, tick-tock hours. Catch all the
> flit-flit birds, eat the offer-food, ride over clop-clop land,
> our great holds-us-up, wear-a-crown kingdom.

Getting acquainted with the place of knowing, the new silent "kingdom" I had been taken to, was an inward process. It took time to clear. Often the insights were offered by the night for me to waken to, usually in the form of poetry like my childness poem. By now I realized that instead of poems *about* experience, I had been getting poems that *are* experience.

In poems from the night I was learning, but with limited access, about death:

WHEN I DIED

After the accident when I died
I knew only about silences
and how to occupy them with travel and arrival
I had nothing to say about.

Someone else lived in my skin
not sorrowful, not curious
not unglad, acknowledging no hunger
no vocabulary of passions
no calendar of things to come.
Only the pastels of having returned.

So if I now am at a distance
and more and more
connected to night
and wake up with a closed smile
that takes up my wrinkles

it is that I am occupied:
by the light that tells me
where I have been and will go

listens with me in the ringing
and rejoicing of having had the time.

About what happened in the accident itself, I needed the informing and insightful offerings of others, by way of what they know and see that I am not privy to on my own, even when sleeping. Unable to sort out my experience by usual routes, I have often been drawn to mystic connections. Rather than negate or question enlightenment from unlike sources, my Mormon background has lent credence to what I have learned. Accustomed to personal ties to the divine, I have found truth in professional readings offered by psychics, an astrologer, a numerologist, and observations by sound, complementary medical practitioners. Spiritually positive, faith promoting, and full of understanding, they have fascinated and inspired me, especially since all of their findings over the years match as if written in a family history. Totally real and important to my understanding, I have saved them in the stacks of my references as well as in corners of my mind, reluctant, but I know now waiting, to fold them into my book about believing.

Almost forgotten in specifics, they stayed locked away as I wrestled with how to wring from all that was so private—and to many, of questionable veracity—what needed to be told if I was to let be known what I was given in the accident. Finally, nearly eighteen years after my death experience, the blessed night provided an exact description for anyone who would hear, especially for me. As I lay on my pillow that next morning, what I waited so long to articulate came just as my childness poem did: an amalgam of truths gleaned from sincere and gifted offerings—what I could never have brought up on my own. What I now dared say:

Put yourself in my place: a blow to your head—lightning illuminates a view of past, present, and future. In that brief illumination, you are informed. A door has opened. It will stay open for you to be witness to what the light has shown even after the lightning disappears. You will never be the same. You have been to the place of knowing. You have returned with a promise.

The light has illumined you inside, where your spirit

dwells. You are filled with the flame. This is no "willing suspension of disbelief," as acceptance of fantasy requires. This is pure believing, knowing; no doubting. What you have been witness to will never leave you. You will be going back and forth between *here* and *there*, without intermediary, but being led by the light.

You will gradually realize your body is not you. It is a vehicle through which you can animate the light infused in you. It is the manifestation of "let His spirit be with you." What greater gift? Forever that spirit will answer privately.

You will find access to interconnectedness. The flame in you will connect to the flame in others. It is the illumination of the divine. It illumines the space beyond judgment. It is mercy alive. It is love. You will live by this light. You will be given presence in the moment. Every moment will be yours to honor.

You will be a teacher of what you have been shown. You agreed to carry this new information with you as you returned. This will have a profound implication about fear, especially the fear of death, which is the greatest fear for most people. You will open channels between *here* and *there*. Your thought patterns about death have been altered. You can be a direct connection between wondering and the knowing that is beyond description. That knowing is not a literal place, but a state of mind.

Integrating with your body will take time. A lot has shifted in your body. This has changed your way of moving through your world. What you have experienced is beyond understanding. You can access now a new level of information, much more profound, close to oneness. You will travel often between worlds. Your guides will be with you, ready to supply what you need. Go in peace. And let your peace and love be what your spirit will offer.

Was my death experience too private to talk about? Too grand sounding? Too far from the humbleness I now felt in my gratitude for having had the experience? I knew I must not trivialize it. I must remember. It really happened. It was not a dream. I must not forget.

As I assimilated it, this much I knew about my accident: I went away and returned with a promise to keep. It had taken months before I actually accepted that I had died. Keeping that promise of offering peace would take the rest of my life. Love would be the directing force, love that is not finite. This I had to teach. The more we love, the more we are privileged to love: a husband as well as mother and father, a second or later child as much as a first, an adopted country as much as a homeland, a new friend as much as an old one, without abandoning or loving less. And now, what can be learned from a new experience as much as from tradition or practice?

How reluctant had I been to discover, let alone now to admit to, such an acquaintance with knowing? With what a mystic might know? Who in my world would understand or even try to?

The offering of my new knowing was anything but easy. What proof of my death experience? Early on, at the first meeting of the *Deseret News* board I was able to attend after the accident, I even took the six-pound, rusty iron rod that had hit me. After my telling of my accident and my encounter with death, the brethren showed great concern, each saying how grateful he was that I had survived. But about my experience with death? Not a word. Not a question. But at that time, what had I let myself know of my knowing? Let alone of my promise? How could I presume what even my Mormon faith demanded? How was I to embody the message of Mosiah 4:20–21 in the Book of Mormon?

So exceedingly great was your joy. And now, if God, who has created you, on whom you are dependent for your lives and for all that ye have and are, doth grant unto you whatsoever ye ask that is right, in faith, believing that ye shall receive, O then, how ye ought to impart of the substance that ye have one to another.

I was yet to find that my message was not only personal—without intermediary and full of a light I had not known before—but that light was meant to connect with the light in others.

It was beyond me to tell my brothers and their wives, all more unquestioningly devoted than I to traditions we had grown up with. How could they understand?

I had no one to impress. I needed simply to accept my place in my relationship with God and my fellow beings. My mentor Lowell Bennion had taught me: what matters most is relationships, vertically to the divine and horizontally to the human. But if I did share my experience with death, how believed would I be?

In that very interest, I had put away what I had learned. I talked obliquely about what I had been given, what illuminated my waking and sleeping and kept my spirit asking for more. Any explanation through my writing was paled by distance and reluctance to acknowledge the light that had come into my soul. My concern about being believed had to give way to the reason for my being taken to the place of knowing.

Through a new friend on a train, I discovered that, like her interpretation of believing, I had been born again but to a different understanding that I needed to be honest about.

As I settled into my window seat on Amtrak from Portland to Seattle, a sporty, congenial, fortyish woman—young to me—attractive from her reddish-blonde hair to tall, slim, tan legs in white shorts, offered to hoist my carry-on to the rack I couldn't reach. Before she sat down, she offered to get me tea or coffee in the bistro snack car and smiled at my, "No thank you, but thank you."

We sat next to each other absorbed in our reading as we rolled smoothly through beautiful woods, meadows, and mountains. "I love a train," I'd written in my journal and then was proofing the manuscript of this book. She was into a thick hardback. She asked what I was reading and then if she could see some of it. "Of course." I gave her chapter 1 and we both read for a while.

Finishing the pages, her smiling demeanor was gone. "So you

think you died?" She looked down at me almost scowling.

"Yes. I did."

"Did you see God?"

"No," I smiled.

"Did you see Adam and Eve?"

"No."

"Then how can you claim to have gone beyond?"

I shrugged and said, "I don't claim. I did."

"But you couldn't have. You Mormons think you're gods. There's only one God."

"That's what we believe too. Do you belong to a church?"

Now sitting very straight, she said, "Yes. I'm a Christian."

"So am I," I nodded.

"I believe the Bible—every word. Do you read much?"

"Yes," I said, again smiling, "quite a lot."

"But the Bible? You Mormons have another book instead. And you don't believe in the Godhead."

"Yes," I said, "in all three. The Bible is very important to us too."

"But the blood of Christ is the only way to be saved."

"There is a lot to that. We think more of the living Christ than the Christ on the cross—like the Christus in our visitors center with his arms outstretched in welcome."

"We're all sinners, and only the grace of Jesus Christ can save us. We have nothing to say about it—or do about it. You Mormons think you can do works and be saved. I can't wait to see God—and Adam and Eve and ask them why they ate the apple."

"One of our beliefs is that we'll be punished for our own sins, not for Adam's transgression. A newborn baby sinful? And would you want to be living in the Garden of Eden?"

"Oh my, yes."

"With no work, no using your talents? No doing something for someone else? I like to think Eve freed us up to be all we can be."

"See, you Mormons think work will get you saved."

Unlike the train we traveled on, we were on two different tracks, our perceptions accurate to ourselves but never likely to appeal to the other one. So? I wondered how our Mormon missionaries might sometimes affect others. What does it take to converse as well as convert? I liked her. She would have an impact on what I was hoping to write. I smiled and asked, "Do you play tennis?—that tan."

"Oh yes, and water-ski. We have a boat on Lake . . ."

Immediately there was a softening. We talked tennis and water-skiing, then about our families. The tension was gone. We were just two women traveling through beautiful country that was her home ground. Alive in our own convictions, she and I knew different truths, private as our sleep, certain as our knowing what we read and how we believe. Friendly again, she lifted my bag down as we left. As she smiled and hurried off the train, I touched her shoulder and said, "I'm glad to have met you."

I was glad, still am. She taught me again how tricky the boundaries of believing—how often set in the stone of exposure and training. Probably my assumptions about her faith might be as inaccurate as her generalities about mine.

What more personal than believing? Her path was very different from mine, and that's all right. We're all dynamic human beings, in motion. What happened yesterday is over, but we must use what we learn and not get stuck there. Her influence on me was just right.

I knew I had to be clearer about my death experience. Sometimes it takes jarring to see what matters. We can be impacted by one person and often alerted to new ideas even as we reexamine our own. Coming to know is an interactive process. Being spiritually open means not to expect that only external events will guide our lives, nor that we need to give up what we believe, only to think in new ways. It's the internalizing that allows selection and expansion. Luckily, there is no static arrival. If we allow it, the journey is ongoing and reciprocal.

Many of us expect and want "the cruise" approach to traveling and conversation—our luggage packed at home carrying all truth and then with everything furnished. It's one way of learning and experiencing, the way we sometimes need it. Traveling can be different though—traveling with soul, willing to converse with others. Virginia Woolf knew: "[Without soul, we are] inclined to satire rather than to compassion, to scrutiny of society rather than understanding of individuals themselves." What I learned from my friend on the train is that mine is for sure not the only path, but it's the one I know, have experienced, what I have a sort of expertise in so that it can be a guide for me and for others who resonate to it. I realize it's not intellectually explainable, but it's real. And it's not the only way.

I learned a lot from someone different from me. What I knew better than I ever had was that if I were to be understood, I'd better explain my stars as well as my pillars and how they can interact to bring comfort and peace even in dying.

PILLARS AND STARS TOGETHER

Mortality / is your shadow and your shade. / Translate yourself to spirit / Be present in your journey.

—N. Scott Momaday

Elemental, unfearful, I had been at one with my mountain home and my pillars as I am now with my eternal life. And it felt just as natural. Decades after my welcoming thunder in the canyon, the iron spear through the windshield was the lightning striking new light into my world. How might I incorporate and use what I had come to know?

Seventeen years, six months, and fourteen days after my accident I am at the bedside of my friend Edith, ninety-three. She is the last of her generation of pillars for me. My mother, father, aunts, uncles, and friends that age all are gone. It is Sunday morning. Yesterday, she had a stroke at home in the automatic recliner she has sat in for more than fifteen years for our weekly visits. Her only child, Bob, fifty-seven, is on the other side of the hospital bed. He has left his home in Denver to be her tender caretaker for the past two-and-a-half months.

Edith has revived, is sitting up some, oxygen and IV tubes pumping life into her still beautiful, full face and bright eyes. Instead of her robe like "Joseph's of many colors," she is strewn into a hospital gown she would call "slimpsy"; it's falling off her bony right shoulder.

"Hello, my friend," I say as she reaches for me and I for her. Her cheek is smooth for my kiss, her back a round of bone to pull into my hug. I hand her two baby carnations, "Sweetie, to remind you of Chi Omega days." We smile, knowing her presidency of our common sorority was seventy-five years ago and something we laugh about.

She smells them and grins. "And what's for dinner?" she grins again. For all those Sundays, I've brought what we were having at home—her favorite pot roast—or, if we were invited to a daughter's for dinner, a plate from there or a cheeseburger and a Coke on the way, and lately a Frosty, chocolate of course. Long ago, we'd pile her into the car from her walker to pick up a hot dog for a picnic and ride among new homes she called "ostentatious." Every Sunday, I've pulled out two candy bars from Mel's stash in his closet drawer of chocolate for grandchildren. "This week a Snickers and Almond Joy."

"Oh, that Mel—tell him he's a saint!" as she stashed them in turn in the side pocket of her chair.

Now was to be our last visit. Edith had been a teacher of English and a librarian, a voracious reader as well as an inveterate observer of politics and people—national, local, and church. I could count on her astute assessments of what we both invariably thought or felt. In dire political times with Clinton or Bush, she was more sad than mad and often greeted me with, "I'm grieving for my country."

I had known her first as counterpart to my mentor and friend Lowell Bennion, in charge of outlining lessons that our chosen committee would write for the worldwide young women's organization of the then five-million-member church. I admired instantly her insights and breadth. Fifteen years my senior, she became my hero of good sense and daring. In any company, she would stand up for a new idea and challenge an old one. I began running whatever I wrote past her, appreciating her good judgment. Along the forty years of our friendship, we came to know each other's families, fortunes, and frailties.

Twenty years into that friendship, her beloved Charles died on a cruise they loved taking. With aching heart, she continued to inspire students, entertain friends, dig in her garden, and read—everything in sight. But her sight began to fail. Macular degeneration clouded and crimped her vision until only headlines and TV came up. Her legs and her once rapid body slowed. In a fall, she injured her spine but left a rest home determined never to give up living her own life in her own home. Annie, her young friend and devoted housekeeper, came on Wednesdays to clean and do her books and errands. Assisted by her walker, Edith made microwave meals. In her downstairs apartment, a college couple listened for her call and put in her eyedrops. She ordered her groceries. Greg came weekly to do her hair, and Sherry monthly to do her nails. Forever a lady of sensitive perceptions, she maintained. Her head stayed willing to think and her spirit ready to rail against injustice or cheer at the balm of peaceful human exchange.

As she fell more and more often, Bob in his frequent visits insisted she wear an alarm disk around her neck. But her right arm began to go numb and moving out of her chair became hard enough that she opted to sleep there, and often the bathroom was too far away. Unread papers and magazines piled up all around her, but she wanted "reading material" handy. Her toaster oven and microwave showed splotches of Stouffers TV dinners, and her sink held half-eaten waffles or ice cream. Her Relief Society sisters brought occasional meals and good friends came to reminisce or read to her. But after we'd had a good chuckle over my trying to mount a horse when my foot refused to reach to the stirrup or one of Mel's "Melaprops," such as trying on shoes and saying, "They feel fine, but they're a little tight in the crotch," she would recover from our laughing with, "It's such fun to laugh. You don't laugh when you live alone."

That was about the only complaint from Edith. I'd call on Sunday morning with, "What's been happening?"

She'd say, "Two big events."

"What are they?"

"The sun came up in the morning and went down at night."

And we'd laugh. When I let myself in her door, she'd greet my "How are you today?" with "OK—I'm hanging in there." And the only time I didn't get my hug was when "a little congestion" kept her at her distance. Along with settling every problem at home or abroad, we talked often about death and faith. For weeks, she'd been saying she just wanted to go to sleep and not wake up—but . . . and always there was that "but . . ."

Now I am holding her hand and asking, "How are you, Sweetie? You look a lot better than you did yesterday." We smile and I leave my lipstick kiss on her cheek. "My mark of distinction," she says, as always. But this time when she says she just wants to go to sleep and not wake up, I say what I know, "Yes. And what a glorious surprise will be there for you. Are you afraid?"

"Yes—you know, the review of your life—all that judgment."

"Oh, my dear, what judgment? I've been there, remember? And there is nothing but love, total acceptance." I squeeze her hand harder and lean close. Her blue, blue eyes, almost always muted behind glasses, hold mine. I tell her of my death experience as I have before, but now it is as if we are traveling there together. She is seeing what I see; the light that I know will be for her—her free and running into the arms of her loved ones. No judgment. No echelons, only loving acceptance and that world beyond bliss, beyond joy, beyond ecstasy, a new life—childness. Just being, without expectation by others or herself of how to be, simply the Edith of no age, no impairment, no losses, she and all she loves as their eternal essences, recognizable, welcoming, full of light.

"Is it true, Emma Lou?"

"You know it is, my friend. As I know it is. I've been there, you know."
Then I read her again the poem revised that morning for her:

ON THE PLACE OF KNOWING:
THE INTUITIVE TRANSITION
For my beautiful friend Edith

Your seated, static life will be over,
your youth bursting with bloom.
A radiance will take you.

As part of the council of all beings,
you will be exuberant as the earth in the cosmos,
alive, astonishing, beyond aging
and places to falter.

Nothing will now be too late
or to be demolished.
No tiring out of eyes, limbs, or systems,
No years can have their insistent way.

Your awakening will be unbounded
pure surprise.
The light and love
over, around, will suffuse your coming

as your passing wrenches us all
through the flailings
of our endangered species
and hopeful, well-taught expectations.

You will be where sleep and beyond
beckon from birth
and feather the heaviest death

with luminous fingers of knowing Christ
to draw us to where you will be
laughing and weeping with the lightness of being
at last Home.

"With love from your buddy, Emma Lou."

We both have tears. So does Bob on the other side of her bed. She is ready, breathing deeply, asleep.

But how to allow the sleeping to take her? There follows the wrenching her free from the hospital and determination by well-meaning hospital personnel to stay true to their Hippocratic oath, to bring her blood-sugar levels up with orange juice and give antibiotics for a perceived bladder infection. One young doctor even insists that she use her mind to remember who he is, that she met him yesterday, not backing off even as I ask her to tell him what she had told us: "I just want to go to sleep and not wake up."

Finally Bob, a lawyer, refers others to her living will and the fact that she has given him power of attorney. That afternoon, she is released into his care. At home, back in her blue leather chair, she sleeps, but restlessly. Bob's wife arrives from Denver; Edith pats her "Cinnamon," the cocker spaniel she's come to love. That is her last act of cognition. By the time I arrive half an hour later, she seems not to know me as I give her our same hug and kiss her cheek.

Bob and I have agreed that hospice services are imperative. Even with Annie's help, bathing Edith has been awkward and inefficient. She needs professional help. The new hospice facility in Salt Lake offers gentle rest and compliance with Edith's wishes. Because a doctor's OK is necessary and because her doctor is unavailable, we call on a neighbor, who comes knowing Edith as a friend as well as the now-comatose old lady in the blue chair. A short exam and he agrees quickly to calling hospice.

Ever since her sleeping began at home, Edith has been restive, her arms and head agitated, her fists clenched, as if she is waging battle with some resistance. I know she needs to be freed to let go, just to sleep away as she wishes. This has to be the dark before the light. I know the doctor. He has brought the sacrament to her with young priesthood holders many Sundays when I was there visiting. I ask him, "Could you please give her a blessing? To unblock the reluctance that's causing all the flailing? Tell her it's all right to let go, that she has permission from those of us who love her. So she can just sleep away as she's wished for so long."

He calls a neighbor to join him in anointing her forehead with consecrated oil. With their hands on her now-matted but still soft blonde hair, he essentially beseeches: "Our Father in Heaven, please release your so-beloved daughter Edith to allow her spirit to be entrusted to your safe keeping. Let her be at peace." Bob, long since inactive in formal church doings, his wife, not a believer, and I, confident in what would be, join silently in the prayer. As the men raise their hands from Edith's head, her restlessness is gone, her body relaxes. Quietly she sleeps.

Here is the holy merging of my childhood faith and the mystic arrivals I have been allowed into through my accident and experience with death. A blessing and a poem to purge fear and invite peace. Both play into the sweet rest for my friend Edith.

At the hospice facility, as warm and comfortable as her own home, she is bathed, offered gentle turning with fresh gowns and bedding; once a young musician even plays a harp for her. Friends visit, read to her, and play recordings of her favorite music. I know that she hears. I also know she is pointing her slender finger at me as she always did when I arrived, saying an imperative, "Write!" We talk to her and among each other as she sleeps. She is winding down in some intuitive joining of her eternal self, the transition as right as being born and much easier. No violent awakening to her other life, only sifting like gentle wind through trees into the childness that awaits her.

The fourth night, Bob calls me at 3:17 a.m. to say, "She's gone." We both sob. I race to her bedside with Mel, hold her still-warm hand, and say, "Good-bye, my Edith." Little do I know of the blessing awaiting that good-bye. Asked by Bob to write her obituary and having already written and read to her the talk she wanted me to give at her funeral, I feel my good-byes have been said. But remembering the grace suggested in various rituals of burial, I ask to dress her, with Annie, in her temple clothes before she is laid in her casket.

There she lies on a gurney, back to beautiful Edith, her face aglow, natural as if napping in her chair. Of course, the first touch of her is cold, stiff, not Edith at all. But the power of loving connection changes that. As right as helping her up from her chair for a full-body hug that she loved, we slip the white dress over her, the dress I'd bought and showed her when she decided a year before that she wanted to choose what she would be buried in. Now she invites tenderness, not shock. This is a final chance to pat her into the journey, to tell her how much I love her, how grateful I am for her being my friend. I feel her presence. Annie does too. In the pleated white, we are offered acquaintance with the resurrected Edith. She will occupy my Sundays with the companionship and wisdom that will always be in that place of knowing.

I am that young girl again, seeing without seeing, hearing without hearing, going by feel toward something holy, bidding farewell as I did to my beloved grandma, knowing now much more than I did then, to say to Edith, "Angel, angel, snowy angel, spread your wings and fly."

CHAPTER 3

REVERENCE
FOR LIFE—
FROM BIRTH TO DEATH
AND BEYOND

God's hand handing, the voice saying, "Let there be life." And "It is very good."

———

If the accident taught me the beauty of death, it also engendered in me a new reverence for life, beginning with birth. In the twenty-four years since my death experience, I have been in on the coming of fourteen baby boys and five baby girls. Magic! The births of each grandchild were very different from my own deliveries.

I never saw my five children born. Those five decades ago, with each I was alone in the delivery room with a doctor and nurses at the end of hours of labor. After holding my hand through those hours, Mel was ordered down the hall to a waiting room for fathers as I was strapped into stirrups and told to push. Unknowing about possible consequences from anesthesia and exhausted by the excruciating pains, before the baby came I asked for the gas I'd been offered. I was aware of nothing until she and the placenta had cleared my birth canal. Not until she was here did I know the scalding tears of joy at her becoming. Still, at a distance she was held up by the triumphant doctor for me to see but not to hold. She came to my arms hours later, cleaned up, dressed in a hospital diaper, a hand-covering undershirt, and a gown tied below her feet. In ecstasy, I could undo her coverings, count her fingers and toes, kiss her all over, and relish her newborn scent, thanking everything holy for the billion rightnesses that let her yawn, open her eyes, kick, and yes, cry. I would be in the hospital for five long days, and Mel would see her only at an antiseptic distance through the glass of the nursery, held up for him by a nurse in a starched white uniform.

Bringing in another generation, I see it all: this one for instance—the birth of grandson Coulson. Official photographer, in my greens I watch—our daughter, pushing, obedient, in painless response, an epidural injection in her spine like Novocain for a worked-on tooth—the doctor deft, all rubber hands and arms. The father, who has invited me, watching with me in rapture, terror, awe: the coming! The breathless what is "it"?

With mottled scalp, bluish head, white face, turkey neck, chest narrower than the head, arms akimbo, frog belly still connected, for the sixth time, from each of three daughters, nine months apart, a blazing genital boy—lifeless, smooth-clay lavender under cottage-cheese netting. The cord, a milk snake, is snapped and clamped. Syringe into his mouth, all of him dangles as the doctor's big hands rearrange him.

Breathe, little boy! Breathe!

Then the life! His one-inch hands with bright pink nails opening, lower lip curling, tiny tongue pushing out, head back—Waa! Chest rising, knees coming up, feet kicking, arms flailing, a sniff of oxygen from a miniature mask. My forgetting to snap the photo of what I came for!

No, we all have what I came for: the wanted baby—alive and well. No, more—the pure gift: life. God's hand handing, the voice saying, "Let there be life." And, "It is very good."

Still in my greens, I go to make my call. The walls sing, the doors and staircases dance. I try to tell on the phone what has happened.

It comes out, "He's here—seven-ten. He's just fine. So is his mother."

But in my car, my compact Fiesta plum, I turn up E Street to high Eleventh Avenue. I can see the mountains, the valley, the city spangling on a hot July night. On my stereo, Anna Moffo sings the aria with flute from *Luca*. "Birds," I think, "streams and wind songs in trees. My whole life." Not a specific held in my head, only a giant rising and flowing like the tears in that room, that delivery room. Delivery? Deliverance? Delivered? I have been part of what makes clouds or the smell of rain or the rhythm of sleeping and waking up. My skin is the skin of the sky, my traveling flight. My arrival is as ongoing as prayer.

Going home, I will never be the same. I have been home. Where else is there to go? As in my accident, I could move from one world to another, aglow with the reality of both.

Twenty-two years later, I am with that baby boy grown into a trim, husky man. We are on our annual spree to celebrate his birthday. We have been to the cabin we both love. Now a landscape gardener, he helps me plant the clump of birch given for Mother's Day. We drink cold canyon water as he tells me why his CD of Bob Marley played on the plump little boom box on a two-century-old table speaks biblical harmony to him, his five-year-old dreadlocks tucked under a ski hat he has knit. For this day, he is clean shaven with sideburns as bushy and black as the beard he can grow, it seems to me, overnight. I think of his sitting with his aunt's Relief Society sisters, grinning as he teaches them to knit hats like his for women in Afghanistan or the scarf of soft alpaca that he crocheted for me for Christmas. "It was cool, Gramma. I liked those ladies a lot."

After Oreos from the cookie jar, he cleans up the scatters of leftover wood under the stilt cabin, telling me how he loves his job with flowers. He picks up a five-foot length of plastic pipe and blows into it, the hypnotic mmmmmmmm of his Australian instrument of choice, a didgeridoo. I like it. With honed skill, he carries a huge plastic bag of debris to the back of my four-wheel RAV4 and we drive to the canyon gate. Craning to look he asks, "Gramma, where does that road go?" The dirt road takes off from our asphalt one-way drive to disappear around a steep curve of mountain. "I don't know, hon. I've only lived up here for seventy-nine years, you know." We laugh and he says, "Let's find out."

The road is rutted into S turns that we have to back up to execute. Sometimes we run up the side of the mountain to avoid overhanging limbs.

"Would you like me to drive, Gramma?"

"No! I love it. My little car has never had so much fun." He's out and holding back branches and bushes, directing my turns. Twenty minutes later, we turn into a clearing high above the freeway where cars have become miniature. And there it is. Unbelievable! A huge, white Cadillac limousine. How in the world . . . ? Unlocked, with the key in the ignition. We climb in, laughing. "It won't start," he says, trying, as we inspect its immaculate interior. Sliding glass between driver and passengers, fold-down seats and plush cushioned ones, room for six at least, a dashboard padded in grey velvet, white fringe around the windows of the passengers. On the outside, small patches of rust run down hinge sides of the doors and the brown vinyl top crinkles.

"Wow!" says Coulson, lifting off the silver hood ornament of the Hindu god Ganesh.

"No," I say. "It deserves to be left intact. We could write a page-turner mystery about this find. How in the world did it get here?"

"Yeah, up that road? Not a chance. Maybe a helicopter?"

We laugh. "And with 2003 license plates. What was someone trying to hide?" What cowardice persuades us to forget to look in the trunk?

Back in my car, we take on steep, sharp curves till the road drops off into our far canyon. Sitting on a rock promontory, we can see over ridge after ridge in every direction, the sunset starting its soft glow into the cobalt-blue July sky. "This is my heaven, Gramma," he says, his muscled arm around my shoulder. "This peace and this beauty.

Even this sagebrush smell. And this." He stands and pulls out his fat Swiss Army knife that we shopped for on his eighth birthday spree. What has become of his scriptures also bought that day—traditional gift before baptism—with his name embossed on the leather cover? Not the moment to ask.

He pulls a leather work glove from the pocket of earth-stained, wrinkled hiking shorts and leans far over our boulder seat to cut off a tall, thorny bouquet of elegant wispy, pink thistles. "To remember our spiritual adventure," he smiles, holding it for me. His Birkenstock sandals balance his dusty bare feet on the high edge I could never now dare with my dizziness. He bows his dark head to my white one and kisses me on the cheek.

In that moment, we hold easily between us the balance of earth and sky. Our laughter, his and mine, is a multiple of the day he was born; my skin is the skin of the sky, the view from the mountain an ongoing prayer.

No, I never could have imagined this Coulson any more than I could have willed his becoming—hardly what I might have pictured of that newborn baby boy as I held him exultantly that long-ago birthing day. Discoveries, surprises, and concerns had sprouted watching him grow from Eagle Scout to free spirit operating a ski lift with a current girlfriend from the Czech Republic. His choices, so different from family tradition, could worry Mel even more than me, but that day he was mine to love and adventure with. Coming down, we smiled and saluted the white limo in its clearing, its small mystery a shared secret for remembering on any of his birthdays yet to come.

Each baby I have given birth to, or been privileged to hold as mother, grandmother, and now great-grandmother, has furnished me the joy of belonging—my substantive spirituality. I have felt the connections to God even as I have known so intimately my human connections to family. At the time of the accident, I was sixty-two, a Mormon housewife, and a poet/writer who, for all of my life, had had to write. Mine was a culture unused to sustaining the two identities in any one woman. Mothers were encouraged, almost by edict, to stay in the home and not to pursue professions or work that would take us away from our children. Even those of us on general boards of the church, sent on weekend assignments around the country or abroad, were expected to leave casseroles in the freezer and clean clothes in drawers and closets to keep our families well fed and dressed in our absence.

Church work was regarded as very different than work outside the home. In the six years that I traveled and put in thirty hours a week writing lessons and preparing for meetings and programs for the youth of the church, those who observed my absence praised Mel for being such a fine help when I was gone and our children for giving such hearty support to my necessary time apart. Few would have regarded time away writing or seeing my agent in New York (let alone an opera trip with a friend) as anything but pure self-indulgence.

In pioneer days, Eliza R. Snow, esteemed Mormon poet, was accepted not only as a writer but as a leader—even called a priestess—but had no family obligations, even as she knew favor as a celestial wife of two of our earliest Mormon prophets, Joseph Smith and, after his death, Brigham Young. Most Mormon women, as Irish poet Eavan Boland talks about, "Like it or not . . . existed in a mesh, a web, a labyrinth of expectations." My culture idolized the simplified woman, ardent and singular, bent to the collective and determined to serve it, the radiant motherhood and supportive giving that I had been mostly a part of for nearly forty years. It was not something I would abandon. But a concomitant life beckoned, the life of those poets. The great human dichotomy: how could I live both lives and be fulfilled without sometimes neglecting either—mostly by being tired in the morning? Luckily, I almost always had more energy than time.

But my mothering has been as unorthodox as my mother's was traditional. Being out of our home almost as much as in it, I have ridden that wild horse to fulfill outrageous, self-imposed demands. I've loved people and causes, speaking for and against. I have thrived on family in the kitchen and on the boat, on caring about each other enough to travel and play together and still understand the need for solitude. My choices have been made with zest, even as they have sometimes been hard for me and the people I love most. There have been gifts but also prices to pay for having a mother with a life of her own—my children feeling sometimes neglected and my remorse over what seemed necessary neglect.

At the same time, they have always cheered and sorrowed for me as I have for them. Without planning it, I may have been for them a role model to endorse in their later lives. My daughters have become women who are self-defining, imaginative, loving, believing in their own ways, and responsible. We have learned together that we are always loved. We relish this knowing.

My Mormon faith thrives on and uses as a missionary tool the axiom, "Families are forever." Marrying, as Mel and I did, in one of the now more than 150 Mormon temples throughout the world, invites joining for "time and all eternity." In my church, being single, by choice or circumstance, can feel like being on the outside looking in while waiting for "an eternal partner on the other side." For me, being married and being a mother has had little to do with edict and everything to do with what I grew up loving and still love—a family. Every day, I remember what my matriarch grandmothers and my mother taught me: to let my five daughters grow up as I did, "With love, Mother."

To have been in on the lives of those five with Mel has been my most transcendent experience—by far. As babies, they were warm-blooded, huggable versions of what my dolls had been as my best friend or cousin and I played with them by the hour in my childhood. Though tired sometimes beyond exhaustion, being up in the night with that baby, at first for feeding—the intimacy of just us—then years later for late-night conversation—with just us—was beyond privilege. Though he helped generously with changing a baby or celebrating a birthday when he was home, in those years, Mel was in on their lives at home mostly as a visitor for dinner, a gentle, smiling man at the piano or organ playing "Polly" to dance to or hymns to march to around the Christmas tree. He often said that being a realtor had all of the demands and none of the privileges of being a doctor—appointments on Sundays and holidays and often at night.

In addition, he taught real estate classes two nights a week to augment his earnings and satisfy his thwarted training to be a professor of history. He needed his sleep. We were busy and a good team, going to church, enjoying vacations with family and friends, and being in tune with keeping a home if not a checkbook. Through schedules, crises, repetitive housework, and homework, I have been tired but never bored with mothering. If anything, it has gone too fast. And I have needed much less sleep than Mel.

At the same time, I realize I could never have not had a life of my own. As with my two grandmothers when they raised their families, my blood has run with a thousand interests and joys. Almost always I have loved my life. But as with any housewife, the demands could sometimes be suffocating. I grew up knowing how to keep the house tidy, the laundry done, meals nourishing and on the table with my girls as my committee with or without Mel. But my high-energy delight in the many and the much could often feel more burden than treat to an adolescent wanting to sleep in on a Saturday or a child waiting to be picked up from a violin lesson. Always believing that quality made up for quantity and that I could love them with all my heart even if not with all my time, I could be absorbed in other interests when they wanted my attention. When she was ten, our poet child ended a poem, "When she's typing / you answer your own questions." Like Golda Meir, I often prayed at night wondering, "Who or what have I neglected today?"

While I'm sorry in my bones for that, I think my daughters have grown into laughing about it, especially as they have become mothers themselves with many of the same conflicts of interest. We have stayed close through great fun and agonizing tragedies, in sickness and in health. They have rescued and understood me even as I have them while I've written about them and been invited into their lives at every turn. Never has there been enough time. Their being daughters of a mother so often claimed by others has never been easy, but when they have needed me, they know I'll be there.

I have just plain loved them. Every night as I kneel for prayer and morning as I wake from dreams, I look at their pictures in white ovals on the red wall above our bed. There the five are, each two-and-a-half years old in a long hundred-year-old white eyelet dress handed down from Grandma Richards, standing with expressive hands across their waists, their hair cut by me with sometimes painfully short bangs that had to be "evened out." Their eyes are full of merriment and wondering, childness personified. Then I look at their pictures with their families tucked into the frame of the long mirror above our dresser across the room. Each time, I go from one to another, aware of the traumas and recoveries of each, their very personal Gethsemanes that become mine. I am filled with knowing that no matter the complexity of my own life, I'm usually about as happy as my least-happy child.

In my prayers, always for each, I've had to abandon my instincts to be a fixer—to learn, as my mother finally did, to be there with love, but then to "let go and let God." Sentimentalist forever, I still have tears hearing "Where are you going, my little one, little one? . . . / Turn around and you're two, turn around and you're grown. / Turn around and you're a young wife with babes of your own." In his later years, Mel has had time to be sentimental, too, watching them leave as wives, or for one, a missionary at twenty-two on her way to France.

TO A DAUGHTER ABOUT TO BECOME A MISSIONARY
For Dinny

Twenty-two, she sleeps upstairs
between the windows of my life,
in the sleigh bed that has housed
the comings of four generations

like exotic potted plants chosen
to color bedrooms with blossoming.
Two high bird's eye dressers contain her,
drawers closed on pink turtlenecks

and speedos, walls of rackets and mustachioed
smiles. Mirrors swing her reflection
of medicated soap and squashed rollers
dropping away from night to issue

a daytime Pieta laughing and grieving,
beautifully turned out, surprising as
a crocus in snow. Other rights postponed,
the child that God intended will wear

the sanctity of the blue blazer,
skirted and frocked, innocent in her
expectation. Of course we have known
she would leave, the covers

opened and closed. It is time.
The horizon whitens. Water runs.
This is morning. She will see. France
will tell. She is changing to

the garments of The Word, will take on
the terrors of the verb To Be,
not knowing yet why departure
spells return. Five hundred forty-seven

and a half days. She will open wide
her arms sweatered for the long cold.
The darkness will lighten and she will become
the waiting room for the willing stranger.

Kisses blow like blizzards through my empty
spaces saying God, please. I go up to sit on
her suitcase that will not close,
press messages into her shoes,

the smell of kitchen under the leather
of her scriptures. Snow has made feathers
of trees. She lifts the sleepy shadow
of her face, steps into the air. She is gone.

I do not dare breathe in the bedroom.
Or move. Only to listen
to the runners of the sleigh bed
following her.

And me unable to make it for fear
of blanketing the sweet shiny smell
of Dr. Pepper lip gloss beneath the down,
above the furrows of knees along the floor.

Prayers I could send and vibes from my most spiritual groundings as almost in a blink those little girls grew into young women and were gone to lives of their own. After each leaving, I was eating white frosted cake and wondering where they had gone, the years, the bounty of a full house. But after the thrills and heartaches of dating and a divorce, one by one they brought men into my life to love like my own, men who invite me not only to births, but to play tennis and golf, and to visits a lot like my brothers and uncles brought to their mother matriarchs of another generation. Always there is the mix of laughing and anxiety over their challenges of hitting a ball or making a living or dealing with the vagaries of their families. We learn from one another. We share the saving grace Mother and Father bequeathed me and my brothers, a kind of situational patience that can be rescue for wounds, doubts, disappointments, and most inherited or blundering trials at any age.

Things happen and things work out. They come to pass, not to stay. In a home or away from home, dealing with what happens is most crucial to being part of that home. To ask why, or why them, or why me can be the least productive of concentrations. Why not me? Why not any of us? The unpredictable in life is often the best teacher, the imperative of flexibility, the thing learned. And faith to pray not so much for "Please, with Your omnipotence change all this," as for "Please, with Your strength help me to manage this."

It takes time to learn, like Job, that kind of asking, but it can be a gift given, especially to a family in on each other's lives and deaths. The loss of a newborn baby boy belonging to our third daughter and her husband was a tragedy very new to us. I was there in a faraway birthing room with the new baby and his grief-stricken parents, and later at his service and burial.

SAMMY

I

You, Grandson Samuel Thayne Rich, on records
your life less than an hour of March 25th,
your mother's birthday, handed still but warm
to lie in her arms, white blanket touched away

so we could feel your fingers, toes,
your father rub the black wet curls on your blue head,
your blue lips open for kissing,
shoulders and knees soft as seal,

family nose and nails sure as the footprints
on paper the nurse with aching eyes pressed
toward your mother, then polaroids, three,
for your parents to search you out alive.

You before the masks, syringes, shots,
manipulations administered in ICU with frantic
paranatal calculations by the team of six
determined by training and stunning sympathy
to render you right—proclaimed you past sadness, gone.

You, Samuel Thayne Rich, there and later in that blue,
for all but us unopened casket, a jewel box
textured and daisy-spread for burial
on a sunny Tuesday like a child's secret treasure.

II

This is more than an angel cradled
in the blue husk of what has been prepared.
It is Sammy asleep. Do not mistake
my acceptance for resignation.
If I restrain my wanting to cup
his head in my hands and kiss his face,
it is not out of awe nor even grief.
But that this is the time of recovery,
hour of tenderness, moment that will thrum
all moments to the intrepid beat
of his shadow heart, breathless
in gathering me with the other sleeping ones
awaiting the awakening.

Familiar and sure since my death experience, I can recall that awakening as clearly as that scene in the hospital. After the graveside service, his grieving dad and I climb the snowy road to the cabin. I dig a stale Oreo out of the cookie jar, inspect the old tub layered with last year's flies, and blow the bugle to say, "We're here!" Standing beside him, both of us search the pines, the grey oak, the crags, the March silence, expecting birds and green. I say to him, "He's here, Sammy."

"Yep," he says.

My "boys"/men offer tender solace, blessings, height to change a lightbulb, strong arms to open the cabin after winter, and ideas for camping that I never learned. They also have come to understand the need for an annual "girls' trip." Every week we have lunch, any of the sisters in town and I, and find it a treat of girl-talk about issues and books, believing and not believing, and time to catch up on our so-occupied lives.

Our annual girls' trips are a treasured extension of our lunches. Usually we've taken one of their vans, with bikes and tennis racquets in a trailer, to convenient St. George in southern Utah, the beach in California, or a theater week from a cabin in Oregon, all thrifty excursions. Our first was to a tennis camp in Ojai, California, run by a daughter and her husband. We slept in the infirmary, ate in the cafeteria, played on the courts and in the pool, talked into the night, shared our faith as we soaked up the sun on the beach, and determined a trip like this must be annual. Living for many years in four states—our together times being most often with a cast of thousands for holidays or summer visits—our time with just us has become sacrosanct. Nursing babies have been the only boys ever allowed. Willing dads with no choice but full-attention-fathering and Mel know what munificence lies in our coming back invariably refreshed and ready for being thoroughly home.

Our first girls' trip had been the spring before my accident. Grateful to have had it, we felt even more the importance of being together after the accident. Fifteen girls' trips after that, I was still alive to the mystique of Ireland, where I'd been invited the year before with six writers to a thatched cottage on Galway Bay. Mel and I had traveled much. Why not stretch to take my daughters, now thirty-seven to forty-seven and with eighteen children among them, to go to Ireland and come back new as I had? Why not now? What better investment than memories?

We six could have an economical ten days of quiet, just us with rooms of our own in an artists' retreat hosted by a friend on subtropical Beara Peninsula in south Ireland. We used frequent flyer miles, for us a momentary extravagance worth more than any savings. We'd have three meals a day if we chose, in a conservatory looking out on flax and surprising palm trees defining the wind of April. For not-so-young mothers, imagine having a table spread and cleared with no planning or preparing.

Most lucky, we'd have a minivan with a driver to take us all together on the "wrong" side of roads to other meals and little-known scenes. He found for us the green bucolic quiet, plus fishing villages and pastel houses, frugal gifts in village shops. We could sleep in, walk the bog to the strand or hike a ridge in Wellies—Wellington boots furnished by our self-proclaimed "jolly landlady." For each, there was no fussing with hair and faces; outfits were whatever suited the whimsies of an Irish day where, as one daughter put it, the sky moved fast and the people moved slow. We roamed castles and monasteries and went to a Catholic mass in a two-hundred-year-old church. Our souls had time to catch up with us.

Each sister brought her individual yen for solitude, two to paint, others to write in their journals or wander alone in the mysterious landscape, all to read, each to go at her own time to sleep in her own bed. We laughed doing exercises by CD on the floor and cried watching old movies on video. Prayer was as comfortable as talk at the table. Below any surface, thoroughly ourselves, we talked about wounded hearts and private yearnings. Together or apart, we felt the balm of congenial stillness.

What of the mystical did we bring home from Ireland? Epitomized in what our driver—transplanted six-foot-four German Heinz, in love with Ireland—bequeathed us. He drove us on our last day en route to Cork and the long flight home, loaded with bags stuffed to overflowing from the handmade offerings of county Cork, all of us knowing it could never happen again. We were laughing as we often did at some banter among us when he stopped by a sequestered lake tucked into oak trees, yellow gorse, and emerald grasses. Turning down his tape of Irish folk songs and Vivaldi, he said, "Wind down your windows." It was raining—a soft day by Irish terms. "Here's one last chance to listen to the silence." Silence, the language of God, he gave us to bring home.

And for me? At the end of any girls' trip, I knew a glad sadness, sad to have the trip over, glad knowing that as strong women, they no longer needed me; that yes, Mother, we have grown up with love and humor—and believing in a power beyond ourselves. They had, by that spiritual osmosis, come home with what my mystic life afforded me—peace in the present and expectation of a future punctuated by the same.

Through them I can see myself becoming. They are my glimpse at the future. I am born, I grow old, I will die. But even as my immortal soul lives on eternally, the embodiment offered in them will stay alive, each becoming more than I could ever be by myself. And love will bind us like a mystical womb, all yet to be born into everlasting life.

In the birth and exploring with Coulson, in the loss of life for Sammy, in a farewell for daughters gone on their own. In aching and in joy, I live as part of a family at home or away. Birth, death, living—God's hand handing, hearing, "It is very good."

"Lucky, lucky Lulie," I say to myself, to know more and more since the accident the presence of that hand in any reverence for being.

CHAPTER 4

LIVING ^{WITH} ^{THE} INEFFABLE—
IN SLEEP, SOLITUDE, ^{AND} SERENITY

Life is so short we must live very slowly.

—from Thailand

I know now thoroughly that angels abide—miracles happen. Prayer is expectation and fulfillment. *Here* and *there* are undivided except by our inability to see without seeing. Love is eternal—as is God. We are too. For all of my life, I've been showered with these truths. But only in my growing older and growing up have I noticed. Maybe because I have learned the importance of granting myself the *time* to notice them. And maybe because I've found them most often in the ineffable.

I remember looking up that word, *ineffable*, years ago to make sure I understood it when a son-in-law used it in a poem about flying solo in a small plane. *Ineffable*: beyond expression; indescribable or unspeakable. Not to be uttered: the ineffable name of God.

I understood it well. It is the moment before the coming of a poem, seeing a baby born, watching that aspen drop its golden leaves in a wind, the rich smell of their mulch, the song of a stream falling into itself, an aria with flute, or the flight of a dancer. It is a wilted plant coming to life with a drink of water, the disappearance of a bruise, the crescendo of making love. It is eyes holding, accord surrounding a table. It is that region between sleeping and waking, the ultimate access to how. It is a daughter skiing a flawless slalom, another playing a concerto or creating a stained glass window; any one of them doing what I can't—or can. It is the arrival of a friend I have just thought about or the safe return of a dear one I have just prayed about. It was the whispering of my mother on the day she died, her talking to someone, not me, as I held her hand and knew she was about to join that someone. It was what happened to me in my death experience and long return. Ineffable—things we know deep inside but can't find words for.

To visualize the ineffable, I had only to look to how great artists use it. On a trip with my family to Rome and Paris, I'd seen original masterpieces and had brought home reminders. In my studio is a large colored reproduction of God's visible finger touching Adam's in Michelangelo's Sistine Chapel. God's other arm is around the back of the neck of a beautiful red-haired woman, that hand extended to rest on the shoulder of a plump cherub.

Beside that painting are two smaller black-and-white reproductions of Rodin's sculptured heads of women being touched by the ineffable. In Rodin's *The Poete and the Muse*, two female heads swirl from the stone. A face beyond lovely whispers into the ear of a woman transfixed by inspiration, her mouth forming a kiss, her eyes half closed, her poet's hand holding to the shoulder of the muse, whisperer of what could be. In another Rodin, *The Thought*, a head in a soft puritan bonnet rests her chin on the stone from which she is emerging. Eyes almost lowered, she is an electric stillness listening to an inner rising as concentrated as hearing music from a great distance. What is germinating there—or formulating a newly inspired way to be or know or do? What waiting for expression?

What I have come to know about the ineffable has been almost entirely through experience. Here at the beginning of the twenty-first century, bookstores, magazines, newspapers, talk shows have been full of stories about what once was reserved for legend, holy writ, or lives of saints or prophets. Eastern thought merges with Western religion; New Age writings and lectures combine with Indian lore and healing; Tibetan truths become relevant to Christian scripture. Airwaves and television are full of near-death encounters. My own Mormon traditions root me in the ineffable—in visions, in faith, in personal connection with the divine. My upbringing ties me to diverse people and the gifts of the natural world. My death experience informs me as no live doings ever could.

My readings have been varied, often inspirational, offered by friends interested in the things that I am. But reading has been less instruction than reminding of what I have already experienced. The explorations I offer here are my private spiritual journeys, shadows, word echoes of the ineffable that I have known and lived through and by. Rilke reminds me to "live the questions now . . . and perhaps gradually, without noticing it, live along some distant day to the answer."

I do live the questions. And sleep, both before and especially after the accident, has been my major route to the answers, the ineffable.

Sleep and I are friends. We invite each other to luminous discovery. As a child, I rode that magic horse skyward beyond the apple tree outside my window in the city, or over maples and Crow's Nest Mountain at the cabin. In my adult years, sleeping is as practical as it is romantic. I have studied in my sleep and awakened with answers to a test, with what to say in a talk or teaching, or how to begin or end a poem. I am convinced this can happen not only for me but for anyone willing to trust. Trust is the secret—expectation and fulfillment.

First has to come not fearing not falling asleep. I can remember when I was maybe three having my brother tell me to close my eyes to go to sleep. This had never occurred to me. I just lay on the pillow and expected sleep to find me. Now my process is as self-conscious as my brother seemed to imply. I let my eyes close, my temples relax, and I think of something so delectable that I don't want to part with it. Then I simply slide like mercury into myself, gratified as I might be in drinking from an old canteen. I feel coddled like a kitten finding its mother's nipple, purring. Sleep comes unattended to spirit me off, as natural as opening my eyes without an alarm to morning.

Much as I love my life awake, I sometimes love even more being asleep. The joining there lifts and lights me. What is joy or pain when I am awake translates into transformation when I am asleep. My people, my guides, my comforters there fill me with a cherishing and sense of well-being beyond even what I could offer my newborns. My whole self understands.

Once a fourteen-year-old grandson said, "I want to know what it feels like to be asleep. Every time it happens, I'm asleep and don't know a thing." I liked his wondering. The next morning, the poem:

SLEEP, HOW DO YOU SLEEP?

Sleep, what do you feel like
caressing my tired vertebrae,
patting down my irritated shoulder,
making your way among my busy organs?

Do you ride on bellows of breathing,
coast on capillaries, nestle in cells,
find pillows in pores,
cozy into my cerebellum
telling it all to coordinate?

Sleep, my healer,
are you the silence seeping
into my knowing
by your knowing all of me
and all of what needs be

so that we are willing to let go
in the morning?

Since my accident, I have learned to approach sleep differently, ritualistically, the way one would approach any physical seat of wisdom. Sleep has become a place where my muse, my Holy Ghost, and I meet, where they supply me with ideas that survive my waking to consciousness.

I dreamed one night of the engraved silver soup tureen, with a mother-of-pearl stem on its lid, which sits on the sideboard of our dining room. My father brought the tureen from New Orleans to surprise my mother in 1940. Every Christmas Eve, I still fill it with steaming potato soup, dotted with butter and sprinkled with cheese, parsley, and paprika.

By the stem on the tureen, the lid can be lifted open and closed, disappearing under the tureen like an eyelid folding away to enable sight. When I woke the next morning, I had been given a poem explaining to me how alike were this lid, sliding open to reveal what the tureen held, and the way I meet sleep nightly. Just before I drop off, I relax, as though opening my mind to a feast, to gentle ladlings from what the day and wakefulness and busyness obscure. The feasting fills me with the savor, nourishment, and answers brewed somewhere in councils I can join only at a distance but that are paradoxically as intimate as my pillow is with my cheek.

"Pray at night, plan in the morning," my mother's adage, is embroidered on a tiny sampler given me by a friend. It sits in the window that lets me look from my sink to our garden. My father's saying, "Things work out," is in calligraphy on the wall of my study. Both supply what my childhood did—conspicuous reminders of truths that lucid dreaming allows.

That's what it's called, that delicate space between sleeping and waking—lucid dreaming, the visiting of the Holy Ghost, or the muse. Definition is unimportant. What matters is the impetus to pay attention and take life in a certain direction.

Years ago, my husband would be afraid for me when he asked as we visited in bed, "What are you going to talk about to that group tomorrow?" and I replied every time, "I don't know. I'll have to go to sleep to find out." It took a long time and many speeches for him to trust what the night had to offer me. With some notes or facts in my head and the demographics and personality of the group in mind, I'd say my prayers, and sleep would grant me what I needed. In the morning before the phone or getting up, I'd quickly jot down what I'd been given—no way to remember if not immediately— and then refine these thoughts later into readable notes for my talk. Whatever speaking I do, I could never do alone. I have never lost the humility and sense of privilege to be invited to examine an idea and then share what I have learned with people who want to hear. But without the night and its offerings, that great privilege could well be a mighty chore.

My accident and acquaintance with death awakened me to the vitality of sleep and to the reality of being able to occupy two worlds with equal devotion and sense of fulfillment. Still, one world occupies the other no matter which one I'm in.

The analogy between waking and sleep, and life and death, is ancient. Since my accident, I have learned, too, that each sleeping can be a small reentry into the expansions of time. A Russian fairy tale says, "Do not grieve and do not weep, close your eyes and go to sleep, for morning is wiser than evening." This friendship with sleep invites me, even in a twenty-minute nap, to a restoration of energy and sense of well-being. And sometimes even a glimpse of childness in my going to the place of knowing. Death can become a long-term ally to accompany our life. At every turn, I find this interconnectedness part of a mystical oneness tracing my adventures while both sleeping and waking. Each nourishes the other and enriches the whole.

In a materialistic, noisy world, this kind of informing does not come as part of most learning. In fact, we are yanked away from it by the need to make a living, when that need ought to be matched by making a life—especially an inner life. It needn't be either/or.

Twenty-five years ago, my husband and I attended a workshop in California for business executives. Conducted by an ex-marine officer with upward mobility on his mind, the three days in class were, for me, excruciating. We pounded through exercises in sensitivity to employees and customers, always with control in mind and with an eye to monetary gain. The greatest emphasis was on striving—a day-planner's dream.

While the twenty obviously bright and motivated people around me took notes and thumbed the glossy take-home binders, I fidgeted and fought sleep. At lunch, dinner, and between sessions, we talked business. No one asked a single question about our real lives, even though we tried to explore something of theirs. The only stories anyone shared were like the instructor's—about molding success through manipulation.

When on the final day, we lay on the floor to meditate, it was to imagine ourselves as having made millions, success in our pockets, life shined up and ready on any market; not a word about an inner life or a connection to spirit. Certainly not any brush with the ineffable, and not a moment of consideration for the welfare of anyone but self. Even concern for employees was how to push them to greater productivity by understanding their motives. We had completed our study in motivational manipulation in the kind of workshop demanded by a corporate or political world. Hooray for us.

After the last elegant handout, and apparently satisfied with his work, our leader asked us to write down what we would most like to have in twenty years. He listed on the board some of our answers—so many square feet in a home, such and such a car, trips to far and near, children successful in marriages and careers—success again measured in dollar signs. My answer did not rate the list. I had written *serenity*.

I reached seventy-two exactly twenty years after expressing my goal at that workshop. Now in my eighty-sixth year, I feel more drawn than ever by the journey toward serenity, nourished by the night. It supplies me, invites me, and allows me to abide in the place of no fear.

And then, there is solitude.

The culture I grew up in and love thrives on togetherness and conviviality, even in prayer. Mormon missionary companions are never apart; for all members, meetings are vital; in a ward, church activity is the index of the health of a soul. The church is run by lay members; bishops and Relief Society presidents are called to office from a membership who may be "active," "less active," or, most demanding of attention, "inactive." *Spiritual* can mean works as much as faith and can be confined to proscribed setting and dictum. Busyness and happiness are twins. Needing to be alone becomes suspect at best, antisocial at worst. In my growing up, *busy* was a badge for a "bandolo" of accomplishment, like Boy Scouts wear to display their merit badges. "Idle hands are the devil's workshop" was my mother's carryover from a pioneer heritage.

My culture does not encourage a woman to find a life inside herself. *Doing* is promoted far more than *being*. In a favorite hymn, "I Am a Child of God," words say, "Teach me all that I must do / To live with him someday." Was it changed somewhere along the line from what I first heard, "Teach me all that I must be / To live with him someday"? For most Mormon women—for most women— years, admittedly, have gone without understanding and allowing the rightness of time alone. I knew I needed time alone all through my girlhood and have yearned for it all my life.

Growing up as the only girl in a family of boys, I had a room alone where I could read, write in my diary, and look out of the window to the sky. Only rarely did I invite a best friend to sleep over, to talk or giggle, after dolls or tennis or skiing all day. After dates, in that unheated upstairs room, my mother had my bed turned down and a hot water bottle tucked where my feet could be warm, the nightlight on my foldout desk turned on. My nights were mine to write in my diaries, five of which—all of my junior high and high school years—I ceremoniously burned page by page in the basement monkey stove for fear that my brothers might read them, especially of my secret loves. But I attended college in town and married a tall, handsome, convivial, bright, student leader and believer-without-questioning man, both of us twenty-five. Straight out of the house I had lived in all my life, we went to California for a year while he finished his MA in history at Stanford and then moved back to Salt Lake forever. I was fifty-four before I was ever away from home alone.

I had traveled, but always with my husband, family, other tennis players, associate board members, or as a speaker to be met and housed by others expecting things of me. At home, I cooked for at least seven, was part of every crew, and dreamed of a day between Sunday and Monday that no one knew anything about but me, a time when I could just be alone. When our youngest child started first grade and I started graduate school, I had to do all of my writing between eleven and three in the morning. My thesis would be my first published book. To write, I stayed up all night one night a week to have that extra day I dreamed of. Luckily, I usually could go to bed normally the next night and be fine—that is, busy with my busy life. Mel too was busy with his life as a real estate broker, teacher, and bishop and thrived on the sociability of our time together. We liked each other, each other's friends and families, our children and their friends. But this aching for quiet was for me a siren song in most of my days.

Little wonder that for me coming to solitude held such sweetness, especially in the growing insistence of my burgeoning mystic life. But, as with everyone I knew, there was the age-old struggle—how to find that time, time to feel my way toward more, even than sleep and its offerings. It was not easy. Steeped in tradition, my people expected my presence—as did I.

It's hard now for me to remember the anxiety I felt in announcing my first invitation to leave my family for more than a few days. When I was accepted to study with Maxine Kumin in a two-week poetry symposium in Port Townsend, Washington, I was ablaze with concern—how to tell Mel? How even to broach the idea? I had applied, thinking surely I wouldn't be accepted to study with a Pulitzer Prize–winning poet whose work I had taught for years. How could I do it? This was 1979, but in conservative Mormondom it might as well have been 1959. I needed help.

I rode my bike for seven miles out to the cemetery to consult my mother and father. It was Memorial Day and the roads were clogged with cars, but I could swivel in and out of lanes, drive on grass, and ride up the mound literally under the spreading chestnut tree where they were buried—Father for twenty-three years, Mother for seven. "What do you think?" I asked not only them but the power I knew they believed in just as they had taught me to. I asked out loud looking up through the chartreuse green of new leaves in May to the mountains where our canyon waited for a new season. I could hear them saying, "Go, Lulie. Learn. Be all you can be." I pumped my bike home, alive with curiosity and sanction that would send me into a new life. Mel agreed without any imploring that I should go.

When I told my brother Homer about my plans, he said the best way to ease my absence would be to arrive in Port Townsend under sail. On their boat *Daisy* that he had sailed from Vancouver to Maui, he, his wife, and their daughter would sail Mel, our youngest daughter, and me into the harbor, there to leave me to my adventure and a flight home two weeks later. My first poem in the workshop, an assigned sonnet, spoke of the turn my life had taken:

SAILING AT FIFTY-FOUR WITH A BIG BROTHER

Unlike the bark canoes we made and floated
past the plank culvert in the creek and followed
relentlessly, stooped and magnetized, the boat
today took hold of a wind and hollowed
out a trail across a robust sea as grey
as lead, you bounding after sail and line
and hollering instructions for my novice stay

at helm. It worked, that being told, the kind
of deft mandate irresistible as shock
for boat and me. And now, these three days gone,
I trim that bold connection, plug in socket,
yanking up a current I could ride on.
If by that sweet redundance I'm beguiled,
it's under breakers washing up a child.

The mandate I respond to most in our Mormon temple ceremony is to realize the full measure of our creation. I was just beginning to discover what that might be.

Away for two weeks, part of that poetry symposium, I felt like a schoolgirl on spring break. Being led by Maxine, writing into the night, mingling with poets was a heady introduction into a world I had never imagined. It was like swimming from the fish bowl into the ocean—glorious! With Maxine's encouragement, I learned to hold onto dreams. With one of the poets in Maxine's group, a young connoisseur of the Northwest, I roamed the fog of the Strait of Juan de Fuca and laughed, writing sonnets about it. I played tennis with Robert Haas, an astonishing teacher and later a Pulitzer winner. Watching him try to pick up two balls at once, I suggested he go for one, be sure to grab it, and let the other go till he needed it. In his lecture the next day to the whole symposium, he used this as a metaphor for isolating an idea for a poem. I smiled. I learned from him and enjoyed an eye-opening exposure to other poets as different as New England–dignified Maxine Kumin, tree-hugging, free-ranging Robert Bly, and ardent activist Denise Levertov. I felt laved in luxury. More than anything, I had a room of my own. I slept in a sleeping bag in the barracks at Fort Worden, where my father had gone to be a lieutenant in World War I. And I had time alone. Never again would I be satisfied not to.

What I learned has stayed with me as a compass to where I need to be. As I explained it best to myself in a poem:

THE OTHER FACE OF THE MOON
On Learning to Go Away

I

There is a place for the undark solitude
away from growing into and going under.
You must emerge like the moon from clouds.
You must learn from the tides.

What you remember most of that life before
was a you with a household of eight, running breakneck
into breakfastlunchdinner wrapped and packaged
in Little Leagues, rolls, programs,

the well-being of casseroles and showers:
a you honed by lists and hand-to-hand
combat with schedules, all with overwhelming
accompaniment room-to-room, wall-to-wall.

Despite how you cared for the others
you could have been an alarming
picture against the unending landscape
of feeding and voices, causes, celebrations,

crises, deadlines and bedtimes. And
loveliness. Loving. Play. Even the cabin
a slide in the deluge. But something
drew you back, gave warning:

everything wavers; even the protected
must escape their protectors. What was
waiting to be let out was you. The you
willing to notice, with the audacity to choose.

II

Before you were married, your mother's
foldout desk in your own room in that house
of brothers washed you into bed with what
came from a day, a page, fantasies riding the moon

to make themselves at home. On the best dreamers
nothing is wasted. Half a lifetime later,
beginning to see, you stirred deliciously, knew
that formulas or pharmacies, not even prayers

could have helped you. Only not waiting longer
for the unclouded moon seen only in stillness:
that being between what was listed, separate
from even the kisses savory from mouth to mouth.

You would leave indefinite in all but the leaving,
hostile to nothing. In some room of your own
you would pass time with no one waiting for you,
exquisitely slow, no problem with

the business of eating or answering calls.
Sleep would inform you and morning would be wise.
You would find what was there: the other face
of the moon and stillness.

III

Everything gathered that first time:
away, crisp, solitary, deliciously anonymous,
you flew onto paper, slept through ablutions,

skipped meals, gorged on drifting, a walk,
a bath, a book, going to the end of a thought,
being surprised by light, listening, listening.

But away was not by itself enough either.
Day after day even of stillness told when
it was time you reentered, came face to face

with the intimate detail of fingers and sentences
mixing with yours. Passion started up
for a place not empty of misfortunes, for doorbells

and phones, pot roast and broccoli, you deployed
plate by plate, lucky to be called by voices
to the luringest colors of fire, the sweet-smelling uproar,

the eyes, the skin soliciting, warm,
the moon hidden in the landscape,
you inebriate of their offerings.

IV

As in the moon's cycle of phases
there are stretches that befit
the season. For thirty-one years
you thought by giving what you had

to the one life you assumed you had chosen,
all would be repaid in the currency
of your own blood, voice, approval of elders,
the fancies of small children.

After all, didn't your family explain you?
The others reward in kind? But your obligation

was to sing in yourself as well as to those who called
for your song. No one loves anything always the same.

If the gift of quiescence is denied even the joyous lover,
the spirit contorts in its own unwinding.
Finding your way away you did no harm except perhaps
to the death of that spirit. Whatever you took

from either life you raised up in the other
alongside spines stronger, shining cheeks not ever
forgotten, flourishings in your departures, sure
of your hungering to return. You alive and paying

attention. Your pages wait to be finished,
may never be. But stillness plays on the other face
of the moon, and you, restive and calm, hang tough
between phases, knowing when to let it be.

Going away to solitude became a passion—two weeks twice a year. First, Maxine invited me to stay on the farm she and her husband had retired to in New Hampshire. "Write!" she admonished me, unable to imagine the life of a Salt Lake Mormon woman—with grown children, no less—who could find no space to do what so compelled her. I went six times. Then, with her urging and Henry Taylor's— earlier, chairman of my master's committee and later, winner of a Pulitzer—I went for three or even four weeks to artists' retreats in Virginia, Illinois, and Florida, accepted and paying only ten dollars a day. I felt sponsored by the Medici.

From my painter friends, I learned I could not work effectively at my cluttered desk in our basement. I needed my "north light." By usual luck, some pals had a vacant little house behind their big house that had earlier housed their eight children. It became my studio for fifteen years. Six books later, seven minutes from home, with no phone and no one coming, it continued as my refuge, the closest thing to solitude in my city that I ever could have concocted. I still have the wonder of another studio a little farther away.

But life drew me in a thousand directions. When longtime friends in Sun Valley, Idaho, offered me their empty condo in off seasons—October and April—leaving town alone became a tantalizing option. Identity in marriage can't be always as one. Mel's support emotionally as well as financially had forever lent me a freedom I blessed and thrived on. Though he had been my most enthusiastic fan, convincing him of the critical importance of my time away and alone was not easy. Who did we know who took such vacations from responsibility? I had to convince him that my life was literally at stake, my inner life. Writing was like breathing, like his working life was to him. But what would people think? "If you or one of my brothers had to be away for your job, would anyone question the rightness of it? Feel sorry for the poor wife left at home?" Such a premise was untried in our neck of the woods.

It took cultivating approval through explaining everywhere—to neighbors, friends, relatives, boards—for my going away to be deemed all right. Foolishness! Surely only neglect at home could be fostered by time away. What Mel and I found after the initial trauma of making the time was that spaces in our togetherness ripened our relishing time together. Our daughters, in their often hectic lives understood and came to finding some time themselves to plumb their own inner spiritual informings. One wrote me after a night at my studio, "Thank you, Mom, for sharing your quiet place, and thank you for passing down the need for solitude. I love you."

During this time, women friends started going to school and taking jobs in government, nursing, real estate, and education. Once when the *Deseret News* board summer party was at our cabin, the men in the meeting just hours before talked of picking up their wives to come. In the big leather armchair in the boardroom (where my shortness had either to dangle or slouch to touch the floor), I mentally scrambled to be ready for their arrival. I joked the old joke of the time, "I need a wife!" New to the idea of a wife's being anything but at home with dinner on the table, they all laughed.

But for me, the lone woman at the meeting, living two lives, at home and away, was epitomized in my being at that long, heavy table where general authorities of the Mormon Church met. Considering bottom lines, news content, and salaries for a staff I came to know and respect was just a different challenge than work parties at home or pulling weeds or helping with a school project. Just as I could multitask while talking on the phone—making a meal, washing down fingerprints on a cupboard, surveying headlines of the day's papers, planning a night out with Mel—I could feel a contributing part to the multiple parts of my multiple lives. I liked it and the diverse people who occupied those lives.

Still, it has never been easy paying attention to all that intrigues and fills me. And it certainly has not been easy on those who sustain me along the way. Thank goodness they've been loving and forgiving, often in wondering just which slot they might fit into for attention. And thank goodness for the laughing we have managed to indulge in in the tightest times.

Maybe it's worked for me by compartmentalizing in order to be present in the moment at hand. Never do I feel uninterested or uninformed by that moment. And never phony in giving of myself to whatever person or cause occupies that space. But now my point of fatigue is changing. Mornings are bright; afternoons can get a bit dim; evenings are harder to stay awake for. One very hot summer, two tall candles in tall candlesticks on our dining-room sideboard melted. One bent over in a lengthy comma, the other clear to the shiny surface. I added a new straight one, and the three became an exact metaphor for my energy on any given day—morning, afternoon, and evening—a perfect visual aid for a talk on aging.

But those hours between 11:00 p.m. and 1:00 a.m. still beg for filling. Sleep stays at bay until I have that quiet time to read, think, listen to music and muses, write in my journal, as Mel, fascinated, watches a fourth or fifth repeat of the news as he reads histories, news magazines, and the papers. His being steeped in knowledge makes him a splendid reference for me and others at meals or on trips. He stays a current and comfortable companion and good company in any company.

Gradually, we made peace with my going for time apart, as he learned to find enjoyment too, in a new kind of retirement—in spending more time with his children and grandchildren, performing marriages in the Salt Lake temple, writing his personal history that I'd feed into the computer, gardening, reading, doing his church work, sometimes driving in any direction that suited his fancy—and his idea of thrift. In our respective offices, now possible since our girls have married and left their rooms empty, we pay bills, try to keep up on correspondence, make calls, and add to our libraries of books that we love. Both of us have matured into a time of growing into who we are. Though he is sometimes lonely when I'm away, we have discovered new satisfaction in being together after times apart. We have traveled the world and relished time alone as well as with family and friends at the cabin, never closer or more at ease with ourselves and each other.

Little could I have known the rapture of real solitude, now not a threat to anyone. Once my seven-year-old granddaughter and I were talking about thinking. She said:

Grandma Grey, you know what I think? There's a little man inside my head and he lives in a little house, and that little man lives in a little house inside—inside there—and then another little man lives in another little house. At the very end, there's a light, and if I listen and pay attention, that light comes to the little man in the little, little house, and pretty soon it comes to me.

I thought, "Grace, Grace, don't lose it! Don't lose track of that light; it's real, all right." I told her just to remember that the light is there, and the angels are singing and listening to her as they will to any of us if we pay attention. "Don't lose it, Grace; don't lose the light."

Out of those biannual weeks in Sun Valley—of watching spring and fall take over the trees and mountains I walked among—came a quiet, sinking into a spiritual realm I would have thought reserved for monastics. At thirty-two, I had read Anne Morrow Lindbergh's *Gift from the Sea*, smiling at her saying that the saints in their rarefied lives were never married women. Married now for more than sixty years, with eighteen grandchildren and nine great-grandchildren to love, I find that being in Sun Valley promises spiritual refreshment beyond any semiquiet—even at our cabin in the mountains or a day or two a week at my studio.

Here my head can go to the end of a thought; ideas can surface and be paid attention to; and especially after my accident, I can listen to the inner music too often lost in the din of multiplicities. Solitude becomes a captivating focus. I have come to know something of nirvana—"the state of absolute blessedness, great harmony, and stability of joy."

Out of time alone come poems—poems I could never write from my usual consciousness—poems to expand my seeing and, more, to look, as Yeats says, "into that little faltering flame that one calls oneself." Going back to my usual life is a challenge, just as staying away too long would be. Not easy is this hold of the two lives on me:

THE WICK AND THE FLAME
Reentry

Back from incandescence,
flame full, wick high,
to snuff or lower brightness
to accommodate
the crossing of a sill
from ultimate to less,

bewildered pulses run amok:

head shoulders soul toes
fingers feeling for a place
to turn the screw
that separates bright then
from

     now:

     a brilliant having been
     full of mystery and surprise

     from inner feasting
        back

            to the wan approval of sameness
            in syllables and certainties
            of wicks long settled

              in the obvious
unfanned by air that stirs sweet night
like fantasies and rapture

made holy by the shining elsewhere
hovering out of sight.

    Making peace with both the quiet and the occupied lives I live has been a sometimes daunting endeavor. But I could never give up either and expect the small glories to continue to enrich my life and let me offer the best of both to others.

| CHAPTER 5 |

LANGUAGE OF THE HEART

Acquaintance with a new way of saying enters the pores, unseen and motivating as first love to an adolescent.

———

Language, whether of mysticism, spirituality, or everyday conversation, is as personal as one's shadow. Learning our own or another's language of insight or compassion is often a rich by-product of letting ourselves be open to what can't be put into words—and of caring to learn. People, geographic locales, the heavens themselves have messages for us, often surprising ones.

We can host newness like a fascinating visitor. "If there is anything virtuous, lovely, or of good report or praiseworthy, we seek after these things." So says the thirteenth article of my Mormon faith. Delight comes from being open to looking and to learning new languages to clear our vision.

My native tongue is poetry, long my natural expression of deepest convictions. My joy comes from being understood. As one poet, Alice Walker, says, "I want to write poems to be understood by my people." I believe that God too wants to be understood and speaks in the language we best understand. A friend, fluent as I never have been in languages, has on her most visible wall her conviction: "God speaks French." Would that I could speak another language than my own. I've learned to trust many kinds of communication—sometimes communication comes through nature and sometimes through what a body has to say. Communication also comes by way of poems offered me in the night. And often I'm given understanding through people very unlike me on the surface. In accessing the gifts of others, I've had to learn other kinds of language. This was the case with Carlos.

He didn't speak enough English to be anything but exasperated at the table when the rest of us—six painters, two composers, and eight writers—gabbed about painting, writing, composing, the weather, and a lot about the unseasonable April cold and rain that had us housebound there at the Virginia Center for the Creative Arts. Sometimes he fumed over his coffee, slapped his placemat with a delicate right hand, flung his Castilian head like a toreador claiming a bull, or jerked away from our annoying efforts to talk, his thin shoulders hunched, begging for someone to follow.

On the road between our residence hall and our studios, even when there were just the two of us accidentally crossing routes, Carlos was only briefly a broad brown smile, one eyetooth missing, his arms a dangle. As soon as I'd try to make conversation he became a windmill of gestures, his head thrown like that toreador, telling me, "No life at VCCA!" And he'd be gone like a stallion spooked by something out of my view, leaving only the air full of Spanish expletives spilling over the loneliness that seemed to erupt out of no language between us.

In a way, I understood. I remembered being in France that summer for the first time, knowing only a little how to read but not how to speak or understand, and wanting urgently to. I lost my personality along with my patience and sense of self and right in the world—all through my inability to convey even the simplest explicit information or feeling.

The most difficult situation was over a table in the French countryside where a family and friends of our missionary daughter had invited us for lamb barbequed in a pit. I had always taken great store in the power of body language—eyes meeting, hands explaining. But in a crowd of strangers with no real language between us, we fell to lots of smiling and throwing up of hands in wan laughter and friendly acquiescence to a kind of nonverbal truce and silent nonconnection.

The worst of all though was that the lamb was gorgeous! The father of the house, about my age, had labored over it, turning the spit over the pit until the meat was perfectly roasted. The lamb, hollowed and sutured by his extravagant stitches, was flung on the oilcloth-covered table, carved steaming with its greases running to two dogs under the edges of the cloth. The meat—pink, succulent from our host's butter basting with salt, lots of pepper, and hot mustard—the meat, thus anointed, was picked up in our fingers, twenty or so of us knights of some odd round table, the feast beyond delicious.

I needed to give acclaim beyond the stuttering of monosyllables and gestures, but it was the only means I had to offer him praise across the table and the abyss of no common language. It was frustration raised to the level of agony. For all my smiling and smacking of lips, for all our nodding and their averted smiles, I felt disembodied, marginalized, stupid. I wanted more than anything—next to being gone—to come to their table again, transfigured by knowing how to tell them how much I liked their "fatted calf." Their children approached me as they would a Martian, a stranger in their so French world; their Guernsey cows munched and, I was sure, were fluent in French beyond the rusting Renault, Peugeot, two Citroens, and the grey laundry hung fastidiously on three lines of very French hemp.

Alienation was palpable up to the final absurd grins, shrugs, and shaking of hands with them as distant and diffident as if we were of a separate species, slightly suspicious for all of our wanting to be warm and grateful. Even with our daughter as interpreter at large, trying to seam us together, I longed for the intimacy of no intermediary. Mostly I wanted to be understood.

Remembering this linguistic helplessness of my own, it was with some misgiving and surprise that I saw Carlos approaching me on the stairs after breakfast. It was his last day of thirty-one in residence, filled, as nearly as I could see, with rage and insult. Disdainful as ever, his hands jammed in the pockets of his paint-smeared jeans, he came on like a thundercloud. His black hair was stringy, his T-shirt sweat-ringed and even from a distance reeking. "Come lunch," he ordered, stopping on the step above me. "Stoo-deeyo treee."

Admitting to myself that I was more flattered than reluctant, I said yes. I would have other noontimes to eat uninterrupted—the box lunch delivered daily to my studio—alone at my desk, alone on the green of the sculptors' courtyard or in the back pasture watching the cows watch me.

Besides, ten days into my stay had taught me how much I had to learn from others there, mostly, of course, through talk—shared talk. So little of that had there been with Carlos, so much among the rest of us—the exquisite and simple exchange of despair and elation over our craft during meals, readings, or slides of our work after dinner in the library; late afternoons of swimming or tennis at Sweet Briar; hiking when the sun brought out six of us and Carlos had elected, as usual, to stay in. To do what?

I had come home from our hike that day thinking where better than on the Appalachian Trail to learn what I had learned? The group of four Catholics (Irish, Polish, Italian, and French, from Iowa, Detroit, Philadelphia, and Montreal) were as different from each other in their feelings for a Sunday as were one Jew from Brooklyn and one Mormon from Salt Lake City. Yet we were companionable as kids on a field day outing, as reverent about mountains on the first clear day in six as a congregation under a pulpit. Talk—talk in the same language—had carried us congenially up the trail to the view and back to ice cream dippity-do-das at the Dairy Freeze on the road to Long Mountain. It had also sent us home with a sense of each other as more than painter, playwright, translator, poet, or maker of music or short stories. We had become friends.

But Carlos, by temperament and refusal to be humiliated by what must have seemed to him spurious conversation, had shut himself away from human contact. So I went with my black lunch pail and thermos of lemonade to studio 3 at quarter after twelve. Carlos swung open the door to my knock with old-world butler extravagance. It opened into a studio fourteen-by-fourteen feet with ten-foot ceilings and the artificial light of four banks of exposed fluorescent bulbs. There could be no light from the two big east windows. They, like the walls and even the floors and woodwork, were completely covered with Carlos's work. His paintings, drawings, watercolors, pastels, charcoals, oils, and sketches were taped up, tacked up, pasted up, leaning up against walls and easels, clinging to door frames and Venetian blinds, covering the table, chair, and bed.

"All at VCCA?" I tried to ask, pointing around, surely gaping in my astonishment. "All here? Done here?" I pressed, needing an answer to assess what seemed an impossible accomplishment in thirty days.

Carlos kept nodding, now smiling. "All," he said. "All VCCA."

Then he was silent, watching me move from a gauzy surrealistic capturing of limbs to a Picasso-like horse of reds, oranges, yellows, the squared mane arched, head held high—not unlike Carlos I thought, as he was leaving the table or even this morning as he was stalking away from me after his brusque invitation to come here. Yet from that minute on, the invitation seemed to have been offered more out of fragility than pride. An altered Carlos followed me, following my eye and my awe through his studio. A warmth enveloped us. Joy in his work made compatriots of a grey-haired American woman with a family at home and a black-eyed Spanish man with relatives, I was to find, only in his art.

And what art there was! Twenty-by-twenty canvasses of surreal landscapes, two-inch-by-four-inch ink drawings of Madonnas. Portrayals of women leaped starkly from among everything else— usually ill-defined, often from the back, almost always unhappy.

"Do you do portraits?" I asked, touching my face and head, sketching in the air.

He understood, shook his head violently. "No," he said, "Only

I love you." He took me to another wall and a large depiction of a heavy woman lying on a bed. I recognized the bed and pointed to the old, single, brass four-poster in the room behind us, totally covered with drawings.

"Your bed?" I asked pointing to the painting, then the bed.

"Yes," he said. "How I dream since boy."

"Is the painting of your sweetheart? Your lover?" I asked, remembering his "Only I love you."

He shook his head.

"Of your mother?"

He pointed about the room to other paintings, drawings, nodding, and then said slowly, "Dead. Long time. Since boy."

Taped to the foot of the bed was a double sheet of music paper, on it another sketch in black marker pen of a woman obviously in pain. Across the top of the page was Spanish script, hasty, full of emotion.

"Again?" I asked. "More about your mother?"

He nodded and led me gingerly around sections of butcher paper on the floor, all drawn on. We stopped at one of an almost architectural rendering of a colonial house, pillared and gabled.

"America house," he said, earnestly. Then, leading me to the table, "Howzes. More."

He opened a spiral drawing tablet on the desk, turning the tissue pages to show both sides of heavy ink sketches of houses, page after page of houses.

"I like them from the back too," I said, pointing to the shadowy reverses of the bold fronts, holding my hand over my heart.

"House—yes. I like house. Two sides," he said holding up two fingers as I had. Sober and tapping my shoulder to make sure I was noticing where he had turned to, he said pointing, "VCCA."

On the inside cover of the notebook a black outline of the residence hall slanted and fused to the same pain in the form of the woman on the music paper.

"Not happy," I said to him, now communication immediate, true.

He shook his head no. "But here . . . ," he pointed around

114

the room, "here—OK. But no more . . . " His hands came up like exclamation points beside his face, his eyes closed as he shook his head trying to find the right word, any word. "No more . . . what you call . . . What do it? Sup . . . sup . . ."

"Supplies," I supplied. "You ran out of supplies to make your pictures, to do your work." I smiled and shook my head. "Little wonder!"

Knowing I knew, he wilted into nodding again, shrugging frustration and relief—frustration at running out, relief with someone knowing.

Why had Carlos been unwilling to talk to us, through the even halting Spanish of three others of the fellows who wanted sincerely to help? Who could have helped? Why for those weeks had he chosen to bolt rather than resolve an impasse? How did he feel about his overall stay in Virginia? Why his abrasive behavior? I'll never be able to know.

But that lunchtime as we stood eating our egg salad sandwiches amid those paintings and drawings, I did know something: that I was in the presence of more than talent; that I was being informed by what art perhaps is all about—language.

Out of the faces of his women came anguish and capriciousness. His stylized Spanish warriors spoke frenzy and futility. From his houses and landscapes poured homesickness and intuitive hope for another day. In all of it was Carlos with supplies in his hand, providing what friends, strangers, kinfolk, foreigners could understand and be brought together by, what spilled over as rage and misunderstanding in relationships that demanded a different tongue.

I tried to ask how old he was. I needed to know; he seemed so young. I tried, "*Quelle heures? Quelle age? Comment beau coups annee?*"—all my rudimentary French to nothing but wide-eyed strain to understand, black eyes questioning and willing, but not comprehending. Finally I said flat out, "How old are you, Carlos? How long have you been drawing?"

He smiled a cloaked smile, pulled a stub of fat chalk from his pocket, and wrote on the only space open, the front of a wooden drawer: "35." He looked at me pleased, raised an eyebrow to say, "See I do know what you're asking," and he knew too, I think, that I was surprised he wasn't twenty.

Then he said, "Since one . . ." he put his open palm a foot from the cement floor, looked up to show me how little he had been, said, "My father painter, great artist in Madrid . . . He say, Carlos, see. This how."

He straightened up, smiling at me, the two of us almost exactly at eye level. He extended his hand, small, about the size of mine that he took as he might have a mallet or a chisel. "Thank you to coming my stoo-deeyo," he said.

"Thank you for letting me in," I replied.

Now between us we had a language—holding us together instead of jarring us apart. It was the language of art. It was what has bound peoples and continents and ages together. It is what speaks when little else can—painting, sculpture, architecture, music, dance, literature— the heart of humanity pulsing through conflict and struggle, famine and pestilence, plague and catastrophe, then triumph and love and joy. It is the voice that makes the connections, secures the continuity. If Babel was God's punishment and strewing of the malcontent, expression through art can be the reward—the healing, the restoration of order and community to a world sometimes capable of responding to little else.

And sometimes we need only to be ourselves to connect by means of a language available to everyone.

I've learned through my own experience the difference of language and intuition. Since my accident, that watershed experience with death, soul-changing events both before and after emerge as preparation or fulfillment to color my new perspective. Much of my learning has involved getting to know a different kind of language.

For instance, on November 16 and 17, 1985, a few months before my own "cosmic event," Halley's comet was said to be visible for the first time in nearly a century—the comet seen only every seventy-six years, the one that Mark Twain waited urgently to see before he died. It last appeared in 1910, the year of his death, and was now said to be visible just to the right of the Pleiades in the eastern sky.

Nine of us residents from the William Stafford poetry workshop at the Atlantic Center for the Arts walked New Smyrna Beach, Florida, as we had for ten nights, watching, listening to the ocean. That night we took turns looking through four pairs of binoculars to see the sky.

Naive viewer of the skies, I took my turn, skeptical of seeing anything but the Milky Way at every focusing. Instead, after scanning left and right, up and down, I called out, "Hey!" Near, but not at, the place we had been instructed to look was a bright flamboyant light. I handed the binoculars to the others, and said, "See? See?"

They couldn't see. In laughing frustration, I pointed it out, "Look—see the star, very bright, just down from Pleiades? Now, see the two not-so-bright stars just down and left of that? Now, make an equilateral triangle with those. At the apex of that—see?"

All more experienced with heavens and sighting with binoculars than I, they each tried, wanting to find something as much as I wanted them to. No one saw. "You must be wiggling the glasses."

"It's a UFO, Emma Lou," they said, not making fun, just having fun, yet, I think, believing me. Why, I thought, not just deny it? But I couldn't. Bracing my elbows on a shoulder or the door of a car, trying to pick up the light anywhere else, using different glasses, taking time between viewings—no matter what, I kept seeing that light in exactly the same place.

Finally one said, "Oh well, Emma Lou, we know you come from a visionary background." We all laughed. We were of different ages, backgrounds, and experience, from across the country, selected by William Stafford from our applications we had written for residency at the center—each of us out of our various religious backgrounds, from Catholic to Jewish to Episcopalian to German founders of Bethlehem, Pennsylvania, to my Mormon pioneer ancestors. All of us were alive in our differences. William Stafford, a poetic visionary, grown up from the Quaker-like Church of the Brethren, had said the day before, "In any poetry workshop, we expect to be stimulated intellectually and emotionally, but this is the first one I've been in where we were stimulated spiritually."

The night of my "sighting," we walked home along the hard, rippled Atlantic beach that by day was for driving. Poking up through the packed sand in the slim moonlight, a bright shell caught my eye. Jean, our naturalist, said, "An angel wing. It's whole. That's rare for a driving beach so much like Daytona." I took it to my condo, set it on the table, and went to sleep with it occupying my night by way of my language of poetry.

For the next day's workshop exercise, we were to write a pantoum— a Malaysian verse form I'd never heard of, with the form of the word repetition in the lines following a prescribed scheme. This could sound like gobbledygook, but the effect of repetition of words and lines can echo in the mind to furnish a kind of reverie, even meditation. Letting the words out on paper explained a whole new sense of the mysterious, of what never before had explained itself for me.

MEDITATIONS ON THE HEAVENS

I. THE COMET IS AN ANGEL WING

Angel wings are on the beach
I found one shining in the sand
One late night looking for the comet
We'd been told would be by Pleiades

I found one shining in the sand
A nebulous and luminescent cloud like

We'd been told would be near Pleiades
A long curved vapor tail by the moon's first lifted lid

A nebulous and luminescent cloud now
Striated fragile rippled bone of wave tide wind
A long curved vapor tail by the moon's first lifted lid
The shell as smooth and rough as what we walk

Striated fragile rippled bone of wave tide wind
An ancient icon like the comet's head approaching sun
The shell as smooth and rough as what we walk
A celestial body grounded for our view

An ancient icon like a comet's head approaching sun
An angel wing was on the beach
A celestial body grounded for our view
One late night looking for the comet

Then, just before my waking the next morning, the word *suppose* linked comet and shell to my visionary background. In Mormonism, a fourteen-year-old Joseph Smith—on his knees, after reading in the Bible "Ask and ye shall receive," his heart full of questions, in a grove of trees near his father's farm in New York, had a vision. From *suppose*, a new pantoum came into being.

II. THE COMET IS A STARTLING LIGHT

Suppose he really saw the vision, God, the angel
My church owns the story: Joseph in the grove, fourteen,
A supernatural sight of extraordinary beauty and significance
While praying for a truth that had eluded others

My church owns the story: Joseph in the grove, fourteen
Not unlike Joan, young Buddha, or Mohammed

While praying for a truth that had eluded others
From unusual encounter the gift more than surprising

Not unlike with Joan, young Buddha, or Mohammed
It had to be believed, the unbelievable
In unusual encounter, the gift more than surprising.
Looking through binoculars the night I found the comet

It had to be believed, the unbelievable
The meteor, the incandescent sparkler writing names by Pleiades
Coming through binoculars the night I found the comet
More than white on black that no one else could see

The meteor, the incandescent sparkler writing names by Pleiades
Suppose he really saw the vision, God, the angel
More than white on black that no one else could see
A supernatural sight of extraordinary beauty and significance.

Suppose—a new dimension to believing, another language—
the mystical. After my accident, I had no language to explain
my journey, especially to some closest to me like my husband,
brothers, and sisters-in-law. If they asked about what I was
writing and I tried to tell, they usually nodded politely in that
way that acknowledged we were just on different paths but
headed for the same destination. We simply had our own languages
to explain where we were. Theirs were from the worlds of science
or business, music, homemaking, or sports; they sometimes
intersected mine. But like Mel, they mostly smiled and said
things like "we're just different," not realizing how much alike we
all are.

Later, I read from those who spoke the language as I had come
to know it: "All direct knowledge is mystical. You can never prove
your experience of a color, a form" (Louis Thompson). "The first
major step in a religious life is wonder. Indifference to the sublime

wonder of living is the root of sin" (Abraham Joshua Heschel). "By intuition, Mighty Things / Assert themselves—and not by terms" (Emily Dickinson). As had been true in my canyon, wonder was to be my friend in newly understanding the first prophet of my church, his dedication to wondering and expecting a connection to the divine, and that supernatural sight of extraordinary beauty and significance.

Out of supposing, I wrote still another meditation, this one while in seclusion in Sun Valley three months after my accident and before I could read it back. A new kind of meditation was supplying me. I was remembering a young Mormon girl sitting in church.

III. THE COMET IS REMEMBERING

Not until today this small comet in my head:
The clattering of memory, the painting
In the chapel of my childhood against the organ loft,
Joseph kneeling at the elevated feet of the Father and the Son.

The clattering of memory, the painting,
Backdrop to the hymns, the bishop, and the sacrament.
Joseph kneeling at the elevated feet of the Father and the Son.
Did the artist put it in—the vision—or did I?

Backdrop to the hymns, the bishop, and the sacrament,
My quarter-century there, it rose indigenous as music.
Did the artist put it in—the vision—or did I?
In the Sacred Grove, sun streaming on the boy at prayer.

My quarter century there, it rose indigenous as music,
More real now than Palmyra, where I occupied one
    grown-up Sunday

The Sacred Grove: sun streaming on the boy at prayer
Indelible on knowing, like features of a mother giving milk.

More real now than the Sacred Grove
I occupied one grown-up Sunday
Not until today this small comet in my head:
Indelible in the chapel of my childhood against the organ loft,
    the vision.

Six months later, I returned to my childhood church, the Highland Park Ward, for the first time in maybe twenty years. Little had changed. Through the entire missionary farewell we were there to attend, I studied the famous Lee Greene Richards painting still huge in the nave that I had sat below for twenty-five years of growing up. Only the Sacred Grove was there, trees, sunlight, sky—no boy at prayer, no Father, no Son. Had it ever been there, the vision? I didn't ask or want to know.

———

The group attending that Stafford workshop in Florida coalesced. William Stafford, ten years older than I, and his wife Dorothy, became my friends in believing—about the comet and the painting, the persuasions of my pioneer ancestry, the mystic presence he celebrated in his so celebrated poems, in everything that came ineffably about for him in his writing of a poem every morning. He later wrote:

STEADY—FOR EMMA LOU

It will all escape us if we look away.
It will disappear again into the canyons
that our forebears traversed, praying for
what opened for them at the end of promises.

I drag this wagon because it will connect
all that I come from and that bowl of light
waiting to flood over me. Take my hand
for my sake and yours, and for what this trail means.

One at a time I count over the signs:
mountains, the weather, that surge in the heart
when any turn in the path allows a glimpse
like this, your wagon and mine, and the long trail—

And always for sure: just look at me
and be trusting for what no one knows
till the comet comes for us all in that
vast emptiness we could fall into

If we let go of each other, or blink at the sky.

That "vast emptiness we could fall into" was not what I would fall into. Instead, it was a vast beauty as familiar as the view from the screened porch at the cabin. But it was yet to be for me. Seven months later came my accident.

The spring following my sighting of the comet, my mystic life veered in a new direction. I was introduced to another kind of universe—within myself—and another language. I met Rachel.

Rachel lived only forty miles from me, yet hers was another world, the world of mysticism and psychic readings. I had heard about a psychic's gifts only once—when I spoke at the funeral of another friend, Joyce Henrie. Joyce had been missing for several days. Noted as a psychiatrist for church and civic authorities and a cross-section of people, she had been accessible for thirty years to patients at any hour. Now she was nowhere, had left no note. Her car was gone and her family was desperate. Her husband told me that when every effort to find her failed, the police called on a psychic in California who had served them before. She told them exactly where Joyce's body was—buried under new snow in a remote Utah canyon, a canyon which the California psychic had never seen. I was intrigued that this was possible. That psychic powers could be legitimized as not only extant, but useful by officials as unlikely as the Salt Lake City Police Department, pleased me in its improbability.

So when another friend told me about Rachel in Park City, who had read her with astonishing accuracy, I was curious. I listened to the tape of her reading and agreed that some unusual talent, some access to something beyond what I was familiar with, had to be present in what this Rachel saw. I made an appointment.

A pretty woman with long brown hair and clear brown eyes, slim, casual in jeans and tucked-in denim shirt, Rachel lacked any of the stereotypical fortune-teller trappings. Natural and full of humor, insight, and totally original metaphors, she talked simply like a friend speaking comfortably to another friend about the sacred. As we talked, I felt neither disconnection with my so-long-held faith nor discontinuity with the new vistas I traveled through her seeing.

Her approach to her work as a clairvoyant was through reading chakras—a word I had never heard of—a Sanskrit term for energy centers in the body whose sites, color, and spin reflect progress toward spiritual maturity or enlightenment. Here was a whole new language to learn by heart.

I understood what she meant by my connectedness to people and my being informed by the night and what she said about energy flowing through those centers and the colors associated with them. Like the seven colors in a rainbow or the seven notes in an octave, each chakra has its individuality as well as its correspondence to the others. Energy pours through these centers and creates auras that Rachel saw with her "inner eyes." Then the energy moves through an electromagnetic field around the body to become the aura of the whole self.

This first session needed an explanation of new terminology and concepts. I felt like a flatlander being introduced into three dimensions. Later, I learned about some basics: chakras are part of a Hindu yoga tradition of energy and meditation, similar to the energy theories of Chinese acupuncture and herbs, massage therapy, and Eastern branches of complementary medicine which are gaining acceptance with Western doctors.

The first chakra, at the base of the trunk, is seen as red—the energy running down the legs to the earth, the place of survival. Glands of this level produce egg and sperm, the primal elements of survival.

The second is red-orange, just below the navel, the place of physicality, attraction, balance, anger, joy, and sexuality. Again the glands are ovaries and gonads, but here they regulate emotion.

Yellow at the solar plexus connects a large body of nerves in the pit of the stomach, the center of power, will, creativity. This is the furnace, the fire to do, the raw energy controlled by the adrenals that secrete adrenaline.

Green (sometimes seen as rose or pink) is at the heart, where love and giving originate. This is controlled by the thymus, with whole blood cells that also protect the immune system.

Blue at the throat represents the center for communication and higher will, deciding how to use the energy from the other chakras. This is controlled by the thyroid and thyroxin and controls the metabolism of the whole system.

Indigo at the brow, the place of the third eye, oversees thought, both logic and intuition. It is controlled by the pituitary gland, the rational center and master control gland of the whole body.

Violet at the crown center becomes ultraviolet, white light. This is the connection to spirit, controlled by the pineal gland that secretes melatonin, receptor of sensation. Exposure to light keeps the melatonin in check and can prevent depression in winter. Here is the opening to inspiration, for "inspire" is to breathe in spirit. As energy flowers at the base of the spine, it spirals up through the chakras, opening each. When all are open and all light is pouring through, enlightenment comes. This sometimes jarring rise of energy is *kundalini*, a snake (very positive), coiled and ready to rise. I love the word *kundalini*, its shape and taste, its flow of syllables. I discovered later it also comes from Sanskrit, the literary language of India. The endorphins, those happiness hormones, can be produced by running, other physical activity, sexuality, or childbirth and can awaken kundalini, as can intense meditation.

A seer of the psyche, Rachel was to play an unusual role in the events rushing toward me from my future, my mystic life; as was kundalini. Without planning or any prior defining of it, kundalini had come to me between sleeping and waking, all parts of me at attention yet so relaxed as to melt into the bed and pillow. As with every other process in my awakening to the mystic in life, kundalini has come not from study or effort, but simply from accidental experience. It arrives—no, takes over—as I allow my mind to stay out of the picture, simply to feel and follow. To me, it is not different than what happens to me after prayer. It is the Holy Ghost alive in my body, my heavenly friend, my muse.

I remember, as she sat on her foot while coloring for a long time, one of our daughters saying at age four, "I feel the dots that sparkle in my toes." When I first experienced kundalini, long before I had a name to put with it, this came to mind. I made her words into a verse that ended, "She thinks she needs a Band-Aid cure, but there's not one thing that shows." For me, the presence of kundalini is not like a foot asleep, but a warmth in the soles, the palms, at the back of my neck and shoulders, like a full-body yawn releasing all will. Oddly, it can be watched for but not sought out nor even entreated to happen, just expected and then relished.

So much of our mental space is occupied by reverie, mostly about ourselves—how we did or will do this or that, what we'll do in an hour or next month, wishing, fearing, worrying. Yet reverie can be let free, be used to the nth power, with all me, my, or mine given over. Simply being—allowing the flow of the storehouse of energy in any one or all of the seven chakras. Might this not be one way answers to prayers are ushered through into understanding?

A quite lovely example: the five-hour drive home from Sun Valley, alone as I'd been for two weeks of reading, writing, walking, and lovely sleeping, in touch with October's offerings of yellow, orange, and vermilion.

I was turning seventy that month, and as I drove, a lifetime of decades rose like mountains in the distance. In my willing little car, I sped, through the ultimate comfort of the familiar, toward home.

I wonder if I ever could have planned what happened. First, the highway rolled up over one rise or summit and down into a valley of what was one minute red sand or black jagged lava rock, and the next a spread of farmland plowed rich brown for next spring's planting or still green with a last fall harvest. The earth spread itself flat and grainy yellow or in dark purple-blue mountains, the majesty we'd sung about forever. The sky wore its weather on its sleeve, cobalt blue to ultraviolet brushed aside by white stripes or grey poufs. And all of us in motion.

Even as I gulped up the lusciousness and let the arias of Puccini and Verdi on my car stereo have their way, even with my surges of thank-yous for the plenitude, I entered a different sensibility. As I traveled home, onto the screen of memory appeared one grandchild at a time, all eighteen of them. They came singly until they occupied the whole picture.

Each called up for me an unbelievable affection. I paid attention to landscape, now connected to what would be waiting for me at home. As each child came up in my mind, I took time to study features, characteristics, idiosyncrasies, illnesses, dearnesses, exact times we'd spent together. I'd been in on fourteen of their births, bathing them as babies, their school programs, birthday sprees with just one of them and me, measuring them on the wall by the furnace as each grew past the last magic-marker line, even as I watched their becoming who they were the last time we talked or cried or hugged or laughed or said good-bye. Eighteen of them—including the baby who lived in this world only forty-five minutes—each different. Each, of course, to encounter problems in this life but each full of promise and fulfillment; Sammy in another life.

When had I ever done this before? When this intimate attention to what I loved in them? I never felt closer to them or to their parents who had given them life and shared it with us, their grandparents, nor more grateful or humble or happy. Love flooded me, the car, the music, the fall surroundings that held and floated me. All chakras fed me like the colors I was taking in. I'd forgotten to remember: what we cherish most and what memory loves to evoke are not the generalities but the particulars.

A VISIT FROM CHILDREN ON THE DRIVE HOME FROM SUN VALLEY

You have appeared before behind my eyelids,
*   haphazard as a sky with wind rending the clouds.*
Today you occupied my screen one by called-up one for me
*   to savor against the undulations of October*
on the five-hour drive alone through Idaho.
*   Puccini on my tape sang from jagged lava fields, black,*
to mountain snow beyond the amber acres gone to seed
*   or new-plowed brown lining up with green, unharvested.*

You each appeared for the searching of my seventy bronzed
*   Octobers: grandchildren, eighteen, oldest to youngest*
one by one on the playback of a lifetime running past my heart
*   with the great joy of the visible earth—Nick, Richard,*
James, Grace, Katie, Coulson, Michael, Aliska, Eric, Brittany,
*   Warner, Daniel, Jesse, McKinley, Thayne, Anthony,*
Megan Grace, not quite one year, and Sammy, your life only
*   minutes.*

I am content that once, by homeward fire, I drew your face,
*   each of yours, and let it hold me like an image burnt in*
tile but animate as movements in my womb: that personal
*   your being there, with intermittent rain to rouse me,*
ordinarily a sleepy driver on that long uncrowded road.

Poems went pounding through me like the freight trains
we passed going their other way. Dark lines of birds recorded
your baby smiles grown up and into me with the throb of
you. In my at last unailing eyes you ran to snatch a ball.
On the newly resonant drum of my ear you whispered
the bedtime stories or played the music erected piece by piece
for the memories trickling before me.
In my reverie you offered, each of you, a seeing entirely
new to my life: where winter, snow, November
will no doubt stumble upon me, you will embody the psalm
that will survive through me wherever I stop or step,
where I will not remain alone, but where the earth and I
can feel your company and let the road take us into
the forever tugging embrace of childness, home, and white.

How simple to understand mindfulness and compassion—love of a divine being, reciprocal at that moment as the gossamer ties between me and each individual in my family waiting on either side of the veil between this life and the other to welcome me home.

Two days later, on a Sunday evening, the family gathered for dinner for my seventieth birthday. As always, we laughed and ate and gave gifts and brought our lives up-to-date for each other. Around the fire in our daughter and son-in-law's warm living room were the ten in town of those grandchildren—nine of them boys—in various states of recline, their parents in common states of fatigue.

Setting aside the homemade birthday cards and exactly right surprises, I told them about my ride home. I went from child to child, from oldest down to three-year-old Thayne. I told them what I'd thought about each, every detail. And magic happened. Everyone listened to what was great and unique about everyone else—and especially about themselves—and appeared to savor it as I had.

Here at my computer, I can pull up words and pages from my hard disk to carry on with whatever I want to make happen. On the screen of my mind, I can do the same. As I return from the kundalini that ushers in the morning, I also feel the gentle pull of those dears out there and in here.

Out of one night when I was away writing came in a poem all the people at whose funerals I had spoken. No different from my living people, friends as well as family, they spoke to me here. Almost nonexistent was any distance between. I knew they were there to speak now for me, all of us glad to be there for each other.

I love the idea of kundalini, the colors in warm palms and soles telling of a rise to potential. For this day, directed reverie; for another, dreams. What will come, what will stay—the spirit waiting for me to say, "Welcome."

The comet seen from the beach in Florida became my symbol of believing what could not be seen, not unlike Rachel's reading of chakras or grandchildren appearing unexpectedly on the screen of my mind.

In the same way as they had on the beach that night, when I saw what no one else saw, the heavens drew me into their mystery and magnificence. Eleven years later, like millions of others in spring 1997, I became fascinated with the Hale-Bopp comet that flared and pulsed in our skies for weeks, sending both public, scientific messages and private ones to our earth. Entranced, I watched with family and friends and alone, night after night, as the brilliant newcomer played on our vision of the heavens, our amateur binoculars more powerful than Galileo's telescope that introduced the firmaments three centuries ago.

Also, on Sunday night, a group of us, almost by accident, left a gathering just in time to see the total eclipse of the moon. That same week, a friend had called my attention to a *National Geographic* feature on what the Hubbell telescope could now perceive in the universe—galaxies beyond imagination that shrank ours to a tiny corner of almost nowhere.

I worked that night at my studio, slept, then woke to a poem that left me crying with a joy like levitation. Alive to an experience I'd never actually had—like seeing the vision in the painting of my childhood church—this poem came to me as poems do when I open myself to the gifts of the night, trusting without question their arrivals to explain me to myself. It had to be about all women through time:

RELUCTANT WAKING
Alone at Last with the Heavens

Mother of my mother's mother
is it you who leads me in and out of dreams?
Fills my palms with unwakefulness
my soles with light, my morning destiny
with what the billion galaxies blaze?
Familiar as the moon eclipsed
and ether-outlined in a casual observance
Sunday night en route to driving home,
or the darting colored innards of the Hale-Bopp comet
clearly north-northwest of our backyard
last visible to those who stood Stonehenge
on its improbable landings, two continents
and an ocean, centuries
minor obstacles separating them and me.

Such distance I will travel again
as ticketing and time allow.
But holding only Mother's diaphanous hand
I will travel by the given-in-to offerings.
To the undiscovered inward
that the outward mimics in the motion
of its galaxies where light and Mother's hand
maintain a seeing I attend with an ardor
even love could never comprehend.

The poem, cascaded from sleep, found its way without me. That afternoon, I showed it to Rachel, now my friend of over eleven years. Her response was one I'd never seen in all the times of being in on her astonishing readings for me, my family, and friends. She cried.

"Do you know, Emma Lou, what you've written, what you've been in touch with?"

I knew only that the words beginning "Mother of my mother's mother" weren't written, but given by some compelling dictation. Was it my great-grandmother Emma talking to me? My grandmas, Emma Louise and Minnie, and my mother, Grace, heavenly informants with me in the night?

The next morning, just out of sleep, I had felt embraced in an animated, all-consuming peace. I find no words to explain or define what occupied me, any more than the childness that told me where I'd been in my experience with death after the accident.

MIDNIGHT AND THE DISAPPEARANCE OF WORDS

These times I exist in a world with no words—
not a name not a place
no backwards no forward no still
no edge no shadow
beginning or end

only light
and kinship
tending to any fatigue
blessing my coming to know
the invulnerability of patience
the trust more than a lullaby
dreaming itself awake.

Finally, I have only one language to explain my mystic life to my brothers or others not understanding—that is through stories. For example:

The Russian astronaut said to the Russian brain surgeon, "I've been in space many times and seen much, but never have I seen God or angels." The brain surgeon, who was a [believer]—the astronaut was not—answered, "And I've operated on many clever brains but never have I seen a single thought." —Jostein Gaarder, *Sophie's World*

The comet I alone had seen was of course there for me. But I had nothing to show for it, only a poem born of my own perceptions.

Gentle nights break over me with the balm of sleep, sometimes wondrous gifts of light, and what I must know to know. Like an idea in the brain or heavenly informants in the universe, my language of the heart invites me to a homeland I'm only beginning to occupy—one to which I can invite anyone willing to come and be open to a language of the heart.

ABOVE, TOP: *Warner family (Father, left, rear)*
ABOVE, BOTTOM: *Richards family (Mother, second from left, front)*

| 135 |

ABOVE, LEFT: *Father*
ABOVE, RIGHT: *Mother*
ABOVE, BOTTOM: *Homer, Rick, Emma Lou, and Gill*
FACING: *Mel and Emma Lou, December 27, 1949*

ABOVE, TOP: *Emma Lou with Becky and Rinda*
ABOVE, BOTTOM: *(left to right) Becky, Rinda holding Megan, Shelley, and Dinny*
FACING: *At the cabin on a summer day before the accident*

| 138 |

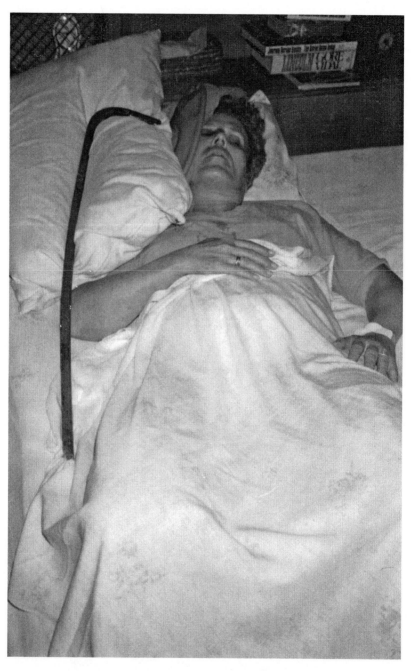

Emma Lou after the accident next to the rod that hit her

Girls' trip — Rinda, Becky, Megan, Emma Lou, Dinny, and Shelley

FACING, TOP: *Grandma Richards's cabin*
FACING, BOTTOM: *Family vacation*
ABOVE: *The cabin*

ABOVE: *Rally for peace at the site of Soviet nuclear testing*

FACING: *Paul Fini painting*

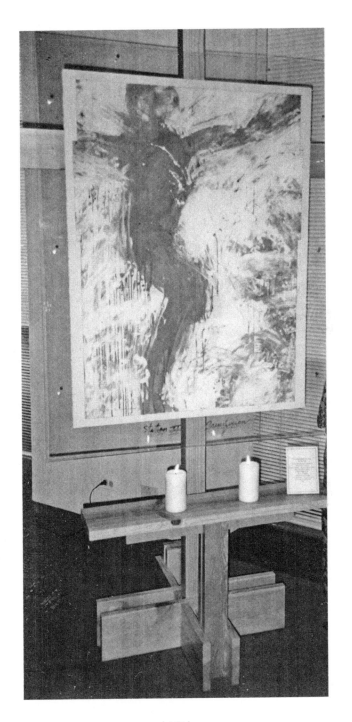

Emma Lou in her study at home (Photograph © Ravell Call, *Deseret News*)

Mel and Emma Lou at the cabin

Highland Park Ward

CHAPTER 6

WHERE ^{CAN I} TURN
^{FOR} PEACE?

Whatever else my life is with its poems and its music and its glass
cities it is also this dazzling darkness . . .

—Mary Oliver

Peace, hardly a frequent commodity in daily life, seemed a natural enough desire for one acquainted with the night and learning to treasure solitude as well as sleep. Peace also was what I sought when troubles assailed. The year before my accident, the Mormon Church published a long-awaited new hymnbook. On page 129 appeared the words I had written while trying to deal with the frightening illness of our oldest daughter, then a freshman in college.

In 1970, treatments for manic depression/bipolar disease and eating disorders were, by today's standards, rudimentary. More than bewildered by our usually happy nineteen-year-old daughter's self-destructive behavior, we stumbled into the bleakest time we had known in our family. Luckily, we sought professional help, found it in a superb doctor and a newly found medical miracle—a simple salt, lithium. She would need it for the rest of her life to treat the chemical imbalance in her system. In and out of hospitals, through baffling efforts at continuing school, as she fought for her life, through anger and despair, she and I never lost touch. For her dad and four younger sisters, the three years of her battle for healing were a blur of upheaval in our home.

During that time of desperation, I was working with the general board of the Mormon youth organization to prepare a program for thousands of teachers of young women. My friend Joleen Meredith had composed music for a number of songs to lyrics I had written. We needed a finale. Why not a hymn? Like our daughter, Joleen had suffered from a genetic depression herself, so I knew that we both understood the imperative behind asking, "Where can I turn for peace?" On one typically hectic Saturday morning, I found some quiet, let my pen find its way and, in less than an hour, intuited three verses with the answer. I called Joleen. She took the phone to her piano, sat, and as I read a line, composed a line. We had our hymn, a hymn that would disappear after that program only to resurface in the new hymnbook.

The peace expressed in the hymn is what provided the ultimate healing for Becky and for me as her mother. When we included it in our book, *Hope and Recovery*, our New York publisher declared it "too religious." But we insisted. What it spoke of had been basic not only to hope but to recovery. It stayed in the manuscript.

The hymn spoke to the longing for peace within. Yet peace in the global sense was engaging me too. In summer 1983, David Freed, recently retired first cellist with the Utah Symphony, called me about an evening of Bach and poems to celebrate "kinship among nations," sponsored by the Utah Arts Council. I liked the idea. Earlier, I had met with community leader Esther Landa and Salt Lake City women and men affiliated (or not) with various faiths concerned about war and the nuclear arms race. I wanted to be part of their efforts to promote a new route to peace.

My thoughts traveled back to the jubilation my contemporaries and I had felt in 1945 when the atom bomb dropped on Hiroshima to

Where Can I Turn for Peace?

Thoughtfully ♩ = 80-100

1. Where can I turn for peace? Where is my so - lace
2. Where, when my ach-ing grows, Where, when I lan - guish,
3. He an-swers pri-vate-ly, Reach - es my reach - ing

When oth - er sourc-es cease to make me whole?
Where, in my need to know, where can I run?
In my Geth - sem - a - ne, Sav - ior and Friend.

When with a wound-ed heart, an - ger, or mal - ice,
Where is the qui - et hand to calm my an - guish?
Gen - tle the peace he finds for my be - seech - ing.

I draw my - self a - part, Search - ing my soul?
Who, who can un - der - stand? He, on - ly One.
Con - stant he is and kind, Love with-out end.

Text: Emma Lou Thayne, b. 1924. © 1973 LDS
Music: Joleen G. Meredith, b. 1935. © 1973 LDS

John 14:27; 16:33
Hebrews 4:14-16

bring, we thought, the end of war and our loved ones home. Why did I feel so different now about nuclear proliferation? I had been part of the "good war" when I was in college, full of the same patriotism and fear that had marched off with our boys to bring peace for all time. I loved then, and still do, the America that rose to do battle with the onslaught of Hitler, Mussolini, and Emperor Hirohito.

Naive, I married and had my babies, expecting that peace to last for all time. By 1983, the world had changed. American involvement in wars in Korea and Vietnam, though experienced much more obliquely, had touched me. Then I read in Jonathan Schell's landmark book, *The Fate of the Earth*, about the peril of extinction in nuclear war. "Before there can be good or evil, service or harm, lamenting or rejoicing, there must be life." I was struck with a new consciousness. I wanted to understand my change of sentiment about any "good war."

Poems came as my answer. They talked about Einstein's relativity and calculating whether we peacemakers would inherit or destroy this blessed earth. They talked about what I had learned in high school biology about matter never being destroyed, only altered; about the college freshmen in my classes alerting me to the morality of that atom bombing; about the right to be born and the right to grow old; about my experience touring Dachau and thinking, "Never again!"; about what I would save. A friend introduced me to what Catholic bishops had written concerning the threats of nuclear holocaust in a pastoral to their people: "We ask you to consider as we have considered." I liked that word *consider*. What a compliment—so seldom proffered—to be asked to *consider*. Out of sleep in the quiet of my studio, I wrote six considerations about peace to read at the concert in January 1984. They would be published in a chapbook, *How Much for the Earth?*

As I inscribed one chapbook at a reading in Provo for Brigham Young University's Peace among Nations Week, Dr. Gary Browning, professor of Russian, commented:

You should take your poems to the Soviet Union, Emma Lou. Poetry is a second language there. People will read your poems aloud. Poets are heroes. And peace is on their minds in a different way than it's on ours.

Two months later, by every kind of seeming coincidence, good fortune, and persuasive friends, I left for the USSR with thirty-six others on an education exchange tour. In 1984, the Iron Curtain was formidable. Getting behind it, let alone getting acquainted with people there, seemed as unlikely in my protected, insular world as going to another planet. But guides Kent Robson and Lynn Eliason of Utah State University were experienced in Russian language, geography, and culture. In that giant bear of a country, I never felt safer for my purse or person. But it was my poems that went with me in both English and Russian that became a second visa to ease me through anything as daunting as customs in Moscow.

The airport itself was like a prison—grey, silent, as if all of us in the interminable lines were wearing rubber-soled shoes. From the high ceiling shone lights in cylinders somehow ominous for our wondering what else might be observing our every move. I showed my passport to a very young, uniformed soldier with acne, glad to see even a blight of adolescence as a sign of commonality. He inspected it, looked at me, questioned, "You?"

"Yes." Who else could it be?

Already intimidated, I made my way through still silent crowds to the stolid customs woman with her red armband. She motioned me to the conveyor belt where my red suitcase lay open. Without a word, she began rifling through my layers of shirts and sweaters, pulling out from the middle three of my books and a photo envelope of pictures. "Take some of your books with your picture on them," Gary Browning had advised me. "Then you are authentic. And your peace poems. Nothing in them can seem subversive—except maybe your mention of God here and there."

First she thumbed through the pictures, stopped on one of my son-in-law Jim asleep with his baby daughter asleep on his shoulder. She nodded, barely. Then she opened the Russian translation of my peace poems and, just as Gary Browning had suggested, she began reading them aloud. Not knowing a word of Russian except *spacebo*—thank you—I watched and listened as she read what I knew to be "There Must Be Life." She kept reading about the birth of a baby, about growing old, about "NO!" to nuclear holocaust. I followed her eyes, knowing where in the text of the translated poems she was. Gradually she smiled, kept smiling, nodding, now and then looking up at me, our eyes meeting.

Finally she snapped the book closed, shoved it back with the others into my red suitcase, smiled directly at me, and waved me on. Relief! And great good luck. I was to find that many of our group had had items confiscated, like art supplies, heels of cowboy boots, even Kotex. The poems would later be handled and read aloud by people as various as scarfed women selling candles in one of the few Russian Orthodox churches allowed by Communist atheist rule in Moscow to a young tennis player wanting to buy an American jacket for his vastly pregnant wife in a park in Leningrad.

Through the nine time zones we traveled in that immense country, the poems became my entree—on the Trans-Siberian Railway, from Moscow to Irkutsk and Lake Baikal in Siberia, through Asian Tashkent and Samarkand. At the end of our three-week journey came a transforming connection.

In her faultless English, our svelte young guide told us of the siege of Leningrad (once St. Petersburg, now St. Petersburg again) that began on September 8, 1941, and continued for nine hundred days to January 27, 1944. The war was not over, but Leningrad was saved from Hitler's plan not only to conquer but also to raze the city. It was the coldest winter in memory in 1944—thirty-five degrees below zero. Hitler's forces pushed to within ten or fifteen minutes' distance from the city but never could enter Leningrad.

Historically, when Russia was being invaded by foreign armies, her climate often served her well as a powerful ally. During the siege, there was no water except from the women who cut through the Neva River. The men were at the front. There was no electricity, no public transportation. Everyone walked miles. There was no central heating. People burned their furniture, but never trees—not a single one cut.

Leningraders tried to cross the ice for supplies, moving across it day and night, not sure how frozen it might be. Food was brought from the Urals, from Central Asia. Art pieces were sent to Siberia. The city was determined to live. Three theaters were kept open, as were sixteen schools and the Ural Hotel. Doctors operated in overcoats and gloves; children's sleds often were the sole means of transportation.

Russian cards were introduced for rationing fifty grams of bread, twenty-five small matchboxes. People ate cabbages, mineral oil, wallpaper, and belts. Six hundred thousand died of starvation and epidemics; four hundred thousand soldiers were killed. People died in the streets and lay frozen, covered with snow until spring, when the bodies were collected and buried in cemeteries in common graves.

I hear all this as we drive to the memorial where half a million who perished in the siege are buried. At the entrance are two pavilions, a large square, flagged in grey granite, and at the center, the eternal flame. Over the trees comes the music of Tchaikovsky, music for the one million who died in Leningrad, the twenty million in all of the USSR.

The memorial itself is understated: acres and acres—twenty-six hundred acres. The mounds are huge but only slightly raised, grass-covered. Identifying each mound are two-by-four-foot reclining marble headstones imbedded with a hammer and sickle and only a date (1942, 1943, 1944), one about every fifty feet. The grassy mounds line two parallel granite walks the length of two football fields. At the far end, against the pale blue sky, barely visible in an opening between the trees, rises the figure of Mother Russia.

Fresh flowers have been placed on the markers. Between the broad stone walks, gardens of roses and peonies flourish beyond the mounds and the tree-lined space. We join the few stragglers walking slowly toward the bronze statue gone green with age—ageless, the Motherland, heroic and humble, holding a broken wreath. Entreating, growing larger and larger, it is almost as if she is walking toward us, coming closer, holding her arms out to enfold us.

Above the forest of trees comes the music from nowhere, as though the Leningrad Symphony were playing, as they played during the siege, every week. At each performance, more instruments lay silent on the vacant chairs of those who had been killed or had died during the week. By the end, there were only three musicians left to play. But they played as if all the chairs were filled. Our guide says, "Hitler could not understand nor withstand such segments of the human spirit called up to defend what could not be lost."

As I walk, I remember as a young girl sitting in the Tabernacle on Temple Square in Salt Lake City on June 22, 1941, hearing H. V. Kaltenbourn, the Tom Brokaw of my generation, talking about the invasion of Russia by Hitler that very day, saying that this would be the downfall of the Third Reich as it had been for Napoleon—so far away, so long ago, so very present.

Now a chorus comes through the trees, no words, only humming, like a poem for which each of us gets to supply the words. I take some pictures and walk alone down the long stretch toward Mother Russia. I see a woman about my age weeding the rose garden. I have to know her, know whose grass she is tending. I step near, ask to take her picture. She waves me off curtly with "*Nyet*," bends again in her print dress, straw hat, work gloves—one white, one black. She continues pulling weeds, putting them into a small wagon beside her.

Recognizing that I've violated the privacy of her weeding—privacy I would want myself at the graves of my mother and father—I apologize and continue to walk. I think about the poem in the stone wall at the statue's base, a poem by Olga Berggolts:

Here lie Leningraders, side by side
Men, women and children . . .
No names, but nobody, nothing
Has been forgotten.

I am moved beyond speaking, the day crashing in, alive in a place of more death than I can even imagine. Tears—for them, for that Mother Russia holding her broken garland of oak leaves, for all of us, thinking the half million buried here are more than all those living in my whole valley of the Great Salt Lake.

I turn to walk back alone, the others far ahead of me. My woman is still weeding her garden. She kneels at the bed of someone. She pulls the weeds, moves the soil so roses can bloom on this longest day in Leningrad. I say, "Excuse me," my hand over my pounding heart. I take off my trifocals to reveal my tears for the mother at the foot of the motherland. The woman rises to my short height, her straw hat a ruffle of shadow above the chasms of wrinkles around what is now a smile. Her mouth says what I cannot understand, her gloved hands what I can. She wipes away my tears with one hand, presses her heart with the other hand, and shakes her head, full of atrocities I barely begin to fathom as I think of the common graves she works her way along.

I offer my hand. She removes the long black work glove of a man, takes my hand in calluses and comfort. I offer her my paltry poems. She reads aloud in Russian what I have heard before, now said as if from scripture, the coming together of women in grief older than joy.

She nods and gestures that I should take the poems somewhere high on the far hill, some official place beyond the monument. I start to walk that way, but then cannot. She is the woman of Russia I came to find. I turn, run back, see her with a friend now, watching me, her plump arms open. We see each other, grey eyes magnets between our uncommon histories. She takes me, I her, in the long, full-breasted, ancient hold, the embrace of sisters.

I am late. I run up the granite walk to where the people from my other life wait, wondering where I am. And I am in the garden standing by the roses, hearing a sturdy grey-haired Mother Russia reading in the sun my words in her tongue, starting with "There Must Be Life."

I know that woman felt what I did. And that had to be what had brought the poems—or me—here at all. With time, what else might we have in common? Maybe even a new perspective on my smug American claims and my sense of being the only right in the world. And what would I give to have her visit my place, learn about my land, my people, my freedom, as unknown to her as hers to me before that marvel of a trip and a chance to see.

"How different," I thought, "the symbolism—Mother Russia from the Russian bear, the Statue of Liberty from Uncle Sam." I had seen Mother Russia opening her arms to offer comfort in grief, contrasted with a Russian bear ready to attack. I had long seen Uncle Sam, a man dressed like a flag, entreating money or enlistment for war, and thought how different from the Statue of Liberty, a woman with a torch above a poem by another woman, Emma Lazarus, "Send me your tired, your poor, your huddled masses yearning to breathe free"—matriarchs about the business of life.

Returning home to champion peace and the fostering of human ties to like-minded people in the Soviet Union, I found my talks mostly received with positive curiosity and friendly enthusiasm. But such topics were not always well received. In a time of peacenik labels and political reference to "the evil empire" of Communism, I found myself sometimes suspect.

After I was interviewed on KSL's *Public Pulse*, our second daughter saw in her dentist's office an issue of a right-wing publication with a headline, Is it true, Emma Lou? rebuking me for no doubt encouraging the daily *Deseret News*, whose board of directors I had been on for years, to cover the widely publicized peace march across the United States, especially as it came through Utah. The phone number of the publisher was listed with directives to call and protest. I wanted to protest the slander of my being quoted out of context from an article I had written for *Utah Holiday*.

In that feature, I had told about the delightful visit of our two Soviet friends Zoya and Odin. In it I had said, "KGB? Unlikely. But so? What would we have changed about their time in our home and city?" My "peace friends" and I had shown them American life at schools, a wedding, football game, symphony, and interviews with state and church dignitaries and had decided that every Russian must have a beautiful voice for singing. It had all been as politically innocent as a get-together of third-grade pals. Should I object to the misreading of the article? Why? Why give credence to the distortion by giving it attention?

Not long after this attack, I was scheduled to talk to a parent-teacher assembly in the evening at Highland High School. The afternoon of the talk, the president of the PTA called to "warn" me. A call to the office had threatened that in the expected audience of hundreds there would be someone watching and listening to every word I said. I'd better be careful. The president asked, "Would you care to cancel?" Of course not! Give up a challenge to tell what I had come to know about people everywhere wanting peace—apart from their government—as thinking and feeling individuals?

That night, I asked that the house lights be left on. From the podium on the stage, I could watch the crowd, a packed auditorium. It was not hard to pick out a man in the middle eyeing me the whole forty-five minutes I talked. He could have been the only one in the hall. Now and then he took notes. Mostly he just glowered at me. He looked as if he were fifty or so, a balding and far-from-pleasant man I recognized from newspaper pictures of protesters at the Federal Building. I tried to look straight at him and smile a lot. Not hard. I liked my subject—and my audience. But it was unsettling, and it did make me want to find out who he was and why he so vehemently hated my report about the people I found in another country.

The next day I took the article, told about the threat, and asked the *Deseret News* board, "What should I have done?" Almost in unison they answered, "Nothing." People with such angry intent, extremists looking for confrontation with anyone remotely challenging their agenda, sometimes try to promulgate their extremes in the Church Office Building. What we best can do is simply live by what we believe and let them do the same.

But ignoring a threat could be no lasting answer to my activism for peace. As I continued to work with the steering committees of Women Concerned about Nuclear War and Utahns United Against the Nuclear Arms Race, I knew our counterparts worked in other nations. Yet peace remained elusive, war ever a threat.

Late in 1986, I was still healing from my accident. I could eat again, but my ability to read was still limited. I was invited by strangers to help plan a unique celebration for peace on the last day of the year. At noon Greenwich time, people worldwide would simultaneously pray and meditate for peace. Noon in Greenwich was four a.m. in Salt Lake City, and on New Year's Eve! Fifty million people in fifty-six countries were expected to participate. But what would that mean in Salt Lake—not exactly a site most receptive to the idea of interfaith gatherings?

Still, I was intrigued. In the home I grew up in, prayer and the sureness of its efficacy came as naturally as hot oatmeal for breakfast. It just plain worked. As I've said, when any of us was traveling, Mother went to the barometer that had hung since pioneer days on an outside wall of some Richards' home; she set the gold-and-black arrows and tapped with her fingernail to see its auguring for the next twelve hours. If it indicated storm—and it was never wrong—Mother began to "work on the weather." Her heaven-bound injunction to get us home was like supplication for the parting of the Red Sea. None of us lacks stories of clouds scattering, fog lifting, even a hurricane changing course as Mother held her silent dialogue with her Maker. Now when all else had so lamentably failed where peace was concerned, why not prayer—prayer and meditation on a global scale?

That dark, cold morning it seemed a miraculous surprise—an unending line of headlights streaming in the same direction. Hundreds of people trekked for blocks from parking lots and curbs. We were young and old, from diverse cultures and walks of life, nearly two thousand of us in parkas, serapes, and furs, coughing as we entered the warmth of Kingsbury Hall on the University of Utah campus. The early hour was proving part of the magic, making us adventurers, part of something much bigger than ourselves.

The occasion itself had evolved without any formal organization or funding. There was no printed program, and no one was announced or introduced. The readers and musicians of sixteen cultures and faiths only facilitated connections made throughout the hall—within ourselves, with each other, and with the divine source of peace on earth and good will toward all that had been so theoretically inherent in the Christmas season about to end.

For about one minute, each of us on the program went unintroduced to the podium, then took our places in chairs on the stage facing the audience. We spoke of peace, diversity, heritage. In the language of their tradition, one by one, Navajo, Greek Orthodox, Mormon, Catholic, Baptist, all took their turns. Between musical numbers came prayers and readings—Hebrew, Iranian, Baha'i, Hindu, and Islam. Percussion—sometimes just a run of bells—indicated a change of mood. After an aged Lowell Bennion read from the Book of Mormon, a twelve-year-old African American Baptist boy read in Swahili from the New Testament.

Finally, Robyn Simper, general organizer of the event, read about forgiveness and then lit a candle on the darkened stage. For seven minutes, the hall was silent, a hush unfamiliar and astonishing for those unused to such silences. Then music professor Ardean Watts came forward and lifted his arms and the whole hall rose to sing "Let There Be Peace on Earth, and Let It Begin with Me." On the stage, and in the audience, we joined hands and raised them over our heads and smiled, grinned. It had all come true. It had happened.

The connections were made. We pulsed to it.

Unitarian Reverend Richard Henry offered a benediction that governments would learn to follow people. And the still-early morning burst with "a joyful noise unto the Lord," as people clapped and cheered and hugged. Carrie Moore reported in the *Deseret News*, "The tie that brought hundreds together in the wee hours Wednesday wasn't mere friendship. It was peace."

I thought, standing there among those participants so like and so unlike me:

> Mother, I'm holding hands with a Mormon general authority on my left and a Navajo medicine man on my right. Here we are, working on the human weather, all of us. With the barometer being what it's been, so headed toward storm, this is what we have. It's what will make the difference. I know it. As I know you knew, and know it too. Like your oatmeal for breakfast, it's bound to make us so much more able to take on the day.

In the year about to begin, President Ronald Reagan met with Soviet Premier Mikhail Gorbachev, and walls began to fall.

By 1987, exchanges between nations were multiplying, certainly among women. Women came to the United States from Botswana, the Netherlands, New Zealand, and Thailand as part of the First International Conference of the Young Women's Christian Association. A year after my accident and visit to the place of knowing, I spoke at an event at the University of Utah held to honor these women. I ended with a poem:

WOMEN OF A DIFFERENT TONGUE

You, women of a different tongue, awaken me.
Speak in the language of light
that flutters between us.
Open my heart to your dailiness;
give voice to your fears and celebrations
as you wonder at mine.

Your family becomes me,
the substance of what you believe
colors my view.

You take me on.
Here, here is my hand.
Filled with yours
it pulses with new hope
and a fierce longing
to let the light that guides us both
tell me where to be.

On May 26, 1990, I found myself the only woman addressing the final meeting of the Test Ban Treaty Congress in Alma-Ata, Kazakhstan. Here was a gathering sponsored by Physicians for Social Responsibility, who had collectively won the Nobel Peace Prize in 1986. I was one of three hundred delegates from twenty-three countries. I spoke from scanty notes I had dashed off out of the night.

Almost pushed to the microphone where only men had spoken, I swallowed hard and began. I said after the preliminaries:

I am a babe in your woods, you scientists, business and government people, makers of films, organizers, understanders of tests and bans and treaties. As a writer of paragraphs and poems, as a responder to your world, I have learned much from all of you. What I have learned most is what newly elected president–poet Vaclev Havel of Czechoslovakia said to standing ovations in a joint session of my American Congress—that our mutual future will depend not so much on politics or even economics as it will on morality. And I have known even more since this time together—it will depend on our connectedness—to each other and to the divine in each of us.

By now, my mouth was sand. "My kingdom for a glass of mineral water!" I croaked. In a second, a man's hand reached around to pass me a sparkling goblet. I held it up in a toast, "To the Congress," I said laughing. "To all of us." A roar of applause, my friends told me later, me too nervous to notice. I continued:

I have met, talked with many of you across tables, in elevators, on buses and planes, in meetings, all of you as wonderfully diverse as the way you extend a greeting or wear your hair. I can feel your intent, why you came, that intent full of purpose—but also full of the joy we all felt in getting off our plane Wednesday after almost not landing because of a storm. Landing to the color, costumes, flowers, gifts, ceremony—festive even in our sober purpose . . . We have to know we have been invited to a *celebration* of citizens as much as to a *congress* of citizens.

In three more days, after our visit to the test site in Semipalatinsk, so like our test site in Nevada, we will finish our journey together. We will go home knowing facts, figures, theories, strategies—and a new kind of empathy for others who inhabit the earth we would save.

I will go back home taking from you and all your so-eloquent labors even more conviction in what brought me in 1984 on my only other visit to the Soviet Union.

Then I read from one of my considerations:

CONSIDERING THE END

. . . I have only one voice, one language,
one set of memories to look back on,
a thousand impulses to look ahead
if I will, if there is time
to consider:
how much for the earth?
What I would keep?

Blue mountains against a black sky,
smiles exchanged so well we do not know
our ages or conditions.
Snow melted, leaves moving again.
In a voice, rain finding its way to the stream . . .
A song flooded with memory, smell of pinon in fire,
onion in stew,
a dancer watched like a child,
a child in flight like a dancer.
Hot soup, hot bath, hot air to take to the canyon,
aging slowly from the bones outward,
time to pick and choose.

. . . An idea, the Pieta, the hand of God, a word, a prayer,
The Word, the earth far from without form and void.
The earth created and not destroyed. If altered,
not back to darkness upon the face of the deep.

You, me, combinations of color and sound,
the spirit of God moving upon the waters.
A child born . . .
a celebration for the end of war.

A new generation inevitable.
A candle, a kiss, eyes meeting. Holding.
Life—to consider.

Then no more considering, hypothesizing, tolerating.
No litmus-paper ending in a cosmic Petri dish.
No more silence.
For the earth?
For the life in me, in you,
I say Yes. Yes, thank you. Yes.
In your breath fused with mine
even ashes stir and glow.
It's time. It's time we said together
Yes to life. To ashes, simply No.

I was too overcome to tell. I knew the talk had not come from me but from the night I had learned to trust. But I was told the applause lasted and lasted. A man from Michigan caught my arm later. "Your speech," he said, "a spiritual high!" At dinner, a woman from the local television station said my talk had been the only one chosen to air in its entirety. "You were the only woman," she said. "And warm. The men were too formal. They didn't get to people's hearts." She added, "And you have the eyes of a mother." A woman from Switzerland told me she had liked my toast. "It took such guts to do that!"

I went home with my head crowded by impressions: breakfast with a father and son who had survived the atomic bomb in Hiroshima; two hours alone (with a friend to interpret) with two very gentle men in charge of cleaning up the Chernobyl accident. One, Yuri, a geneticist MD had tried to warn the government about the danger of the contaminated area and had been silenced. Men were sent to clear the radiated ground in shifts of not hours, but minutes—and with only shovels to attack the heaps of deadly debris.

Both men expected to be dead before the end of the year. After the final buffet banquet, Yuri slipped me what I thought was a scientific account of the nuclear explosion and its devastating aftermath. Instead, when I had the pages translated by a Russian friend in Salt Lake City, they were short stories about family life and death. I cried reading them. Yuri had said to me, "I recognized you on TV—your speech to the Congress. You looked like a mother. I thought you would like my stories."

No doubt for the same reason, I received a hug from Olchaz Soulemenov, the movement's mastermind. This huge Mongol poet in a speckled scarf, hair curling over his ears, had waved my poems up and down to emphasize the need to stop nuclear testing.

A month later came another surprise adventure when Mel and I zipped across the globe to travel from Istanbul on the Black Sea to Yalta, up the Danube to eight Eastern Bloc countries, ending in Vienna. Throughout our trip, a brilliant teacher gave us historical, social, religious, and cultural background as we set out every morning. We visited the gunned-out square where six months earlier, Romanian Communist dictator Nicolae Ceausescu had ordered his troops to fire into a throng of students in revolt. The troops refused. Only his secret service fired, as their leader and his equally despotic wife were helicoptered away to what he expected to be a rescue that turned into their execution. Again war up close, as real as a library and museum of art blown apart by that gunfire in the square where we stood.

Later, I was invited to read from my peace poems to a diverse gathering of 250 people aboard ship—from the eastern United States, a large group of retired Jewish professionals; from the western United States, our group of attorneys, teachers, musicians, and real estate brokers. Until then, each group had perfunctorily boarded one of two buses assigned to us. No mingling. No conversation. Hardly even a glance across the ship's dining room to where we convened as separately as if on different tours. "See if you can read something that will let these two groups at least say hello to each other," our teacher guide had asked me. "I've never seen such a chasm between people."

So I started with a poem from *How Much for the Earth?* about visiting Dachau. Universal connections through poetry and the communion in horror at Dachau brought Jews from New York into understanding with Unitarians from Michigan and Mormons from Utah. As I read, a new kind of seeing began to let us see each other. Leaving the dining room after the reading, people were talking to each other.

"You were first violinist in the Philadelphia orchestra?"

"You taught high school physics for thirty-six years?"

"You had Sandra Day O'Connor as a student at Stanford Law School?"

Back and forth the exchange of histories and then conversations. I read other poems, one from that very day in Bucharest, where we saw the graves of boys shot down in the gunfire in the gutted square. In the poem, I found myself addressing a boy shot in that crowded square with his friends, shouting for freedom. As with my woman in the Russian cemetery, I found the evaporation of difference between us. The promise from my accident had lent me the courage to converse:

IN THE CEMETERY OF HEROES
The Morning after Bucharest

Under the blanket of white marble
you lie in your cradle,
a white marble cross your headboard,
your picture embedded there
as it is in my grey head.

Twenty-one. 1968 to 1989 your years.
December revolt your gift. Of the thousand killed,
more than a hundred of you here
in what just half a year ago was a park.

| 168 |

Above the stiff shoulders of your uniform
your Adam's apple—a man's—
belies the surprised eyes of a boy
bareheaded and trying to smile—
as if to assure your mother
that yes, you are grown up enough
to be forever able and safe.

She takes a wet cloth to the white edges of what is left,
sponges away the new dirt
from this end to that of your marble grave.
In the broken, stiff sorrow too deep
to let loose, she bends in her slim gentility
to pull the old carnations as stiff as she is,
lays them like candles in her left hand
as she moves like a reaper around where you are.

Already planted, the edging of something
like primroses fills the spaces the carnations
might have left, fresh, pink-red in green.

I walk by, compelled to touch her shoulder.
She rises to meet my eyes, her hair a stylish halo
of black and grey, eloquent as her silence.
In the language of women
I press my hand to my breast.
"Parlez-vous Francais?" she asks.

"Un peu—I am American."
We look together at the marble cradle,
the dates, the boy. "A student," she says.
I feel my grandson Nicky's arms about me,
his man's voice at sixteen kidding,
"Don't let anything get you, Gramma,

we need to water-ski."
The woman's son is mine.
I nod, point to the picture,
say, gesture, "For all of us."

She knows.
My husband over there signals
the bus is waiting.
We clasp hands, the woman and I,
our tears from springs deeper than any Danube.
And I know why I came to Bucharest.

Any trips were stitched together with local efforts toward peace. For instance, with my "peace friends," I met with U.S. Senator Orrin Hatch and Representative Wayne Owens (both from Utah but on opposite ends of the political spectrum), who co-sponsored and pushed through a bill to compensate the tragedies of cancer for "downwinders" from the Nevada test site. And one evening, a meeting of about fifty Women Concerned about Nuclear War gathered at our cabin, these dedicated friends of many faiths who worked unceasingly for peace. Out of the night came a poem that told me again the importance of human connections:

TRAVELING

It's about borders.
Out there the land screams at its edges;
that is, people think it should.
So they send armies to shrink or bloat
what mapmakers have drawn
from the yankings of history.

On the borders they expect right
to stay on one side. But it thumps
and howls, skinning the sky
that never stops. It is borders
that suggest, give permission,
invite the yours and the mine
of the quarrels, separate, kill.

A border would divide even a piece of time
into here and hereafter.

But what a traveler finds
is that no one administrates
what flows between people.
Mortal connectedness, as if from enormous wings,
orders the comings, their passages,
the dissolution of borders in light
and the breath of human exchange.

Funny it took taking to the sky, then space
to obscure the detail, to let the traveler know
no matter how real, the borders don't exist:
they're only thinly dotted lines,
like the traveler, herself a small bundle of fibers
poised for passing when the soul
eradicates borders
and anywhere you go is going home.

Increasingly, the light in others became more visible as it invoked healing in me. Through the schooling of my friends dedicated to peace, I was seeing the stars visible beyond the structure of my cocoon of growing up.

At 7:40 a.m. on September 11, 2001, I received a call from a daughter:

> Mom, I know you never watch morning TV, but something horrible has happened. A terrorist attack in New York! A plane flew into the World Trade Center tower and another in Washington hit the Pentagon. Turn it on, hurry.

We did. Just in time to see a second American airliner fly straight into a second World Trade Center tower. In disbelief, we were glued to the television, would be for days and nights. The towers were on fire. The tallest buildings in the world right before our eyes consumed by a cloud of smoke all too much like the mushroom clouds we'd seen, after the fact, swelling up from nuclear explosions. People poured out of the buildings as firefighters ran in yanking giant hoses to fight the fires.

Over and over, we saw the replays, the one tower in smoke, the other being sliced into by a plane carrying how many passengers? Why? How? What in the world? Who could believe terrorists? Hijackers? Our own planes ripping into our own buildings— buildings full of unsuspecting workers about their dailiness on a Tuesday morning? About 3,000 of them in the Twin Towers, 189 in the Pentagon. Word of another 44 killed in a plane likely hijacked, falling into a field in Pennsylvania, probably headed for yet another American target—the White House? The Capitol? Its plot found later to have been foiled by bravery reported on a cell phone, one passenger saying good-bye to his wife as he divulged risky plans to overthrow the hijackers and abort the crash of the airliner before it found its target. From smoking, flaming windows people jumped, one pair hand-in-hand. And then the collapse of first one tower, then the other—imploding, gone. Heat of fifteen hundred degrees from jet fuel, full tanks of huge planes scheduled for transcontinental flights.

Then the waiting, the watching, the closing of airports, the spread of what next? Where? When? Millions stranded from intended destinations; rental cars, trains, buses inadequate substitutes for flying the hoards home. A world suddenly appallingly out of sync, TV anchors bleary-eyed, broadcasting shreds of information, us punching up channel after channel for more, more, more; our insatiable hunger fed by the universal affliction of not knowing. A blast of grief on the streets of Manhattan from a mountain of rubble and human remains—New York: this had been a place for celebrating the *end* of war in my time, streets choked with ticker-tape streamers, jammed with service men kissing jubilant girls.

In the week that followed, our president declared that we were at war, the suspension of belief in taken-for-granted security, mobility, everyday American pursuits of pleasures and palaces. Warnings of more terrorism. A frightful need to peel off the secrecy of who might be responsible. Even Betty Williams, recipient of the Nobel Peace Prize, admitted to an audience of women honoring women of peaceful distinction that her first impulse on hearing about the attack was, "Let's nuke 'em!" In most responses, bewilderment, disbelief, then, "Get on with routing them out, the doers of evil, the killers, and their accomplices!"

Naiveté and trust swelled as we took to "God Bless America" and expectation of strength to overcome. I was a girl again, back on the campus watching our ROTC boys march from the plaza of the Park Building into army trucks singing, "I am a Utah man, Sir, and I will be till I die." Pearl Harbor and war suddenly a reality, any innocent notions dispelled then in four years of lists in the paper: WOUNDED, MISSING, DEAD; stars in windows along the bus route changing from blue to red to gold as those boys we'd gone to school with met the enemy in far-off places like Iwo Jima and Tobruk and Utah Beach. War—now a new kind of war—the enemy a phantom of hate, secrecy, and cunning.

This time our wars would be in Afghanistan and the Middle East, the idea of peace far from popular in an aroused country, my beloved country. And my anger—how to assimilate, let alone personalize the damage of terror to the human spirit? My troubled, befuddled mind wandered back to the Holy Land, to the tempestuous Middle East where supposedly the new enemy dwells.

On my one visit there, to Israel years before with Mel and three of our teenage daughters, I wrote in my journal:

We are in Jerusalem. It is March, and raining. We put up umbrellas or buy too-small hats of camel leather. Some circle opens and we walk into our first sampling of remains. It is a beginning as old as recorded touch with God. The Temple Mount. A golden mosque over the rock where Abraham made an altar for Isaac, where Gabriel swept Mohammed to heaven, where Solomon and Herod built their temples, where Jesus at twelve schooled the scholars, later forgave the adulteress, and scourged the money changers. The holy of holies to three major religions.

In the fine rain, hooded, dark-faced Muslim men wash. A cold ritual under outside taps—eyes, mouths, hands, feet—cleansed to enter the mosque, hollow, chill, bare. Except for rugs and birds. The essence, I suppose, knees and wings.

In dark sobriety, a very old Muslim warns my husband of an arm around his daughter in such a sacred place. What for women in this sacred place?

THE CIRCLE
Old Muslim at Prayer

Feet. These are feet.
This is a place
to walk to. Toes.
These are toes. They
go first. After, the heel.
Toe. Heel. Bare or into
the sandal. Then heel. Toe.
In the shoe that walks.

Man. This is a man.
One foot after another.
Hour after hour. One foot.
The other. One step, sand.
Two steps, a road of dirt.
Three steps, a river. An
orchard. Four steps,
a market. Five, a ministry.
Six steps, a claim. Seven,
grounds. Eight, forward.
Nine, back. Around. Ten,
enclosure.

Feet. These are feet.
These are still
feet. This is a man
praying:

> *Bless this broken and beloved world.*
> *Keep the mountains up*
> *and the deserts down*
> *and the river in its sides. Keep*
> *our brothers passionate*
> *and our women more than safe*
> *and our children's children*
> *full of dreams—*
> *and a way to walk.*

After Jerusalem—after the Temple Mount, after the Via Dolorosa, after the Museum of the Holocaust—I had begun to feel like a *tel*, a piling up of plowed-under civilizations and beliefs and bequeathings. Now we found ourselves in a sacred place of an entirely different order: a bedouin camp in the tent of a sheik. Angular men milled about in *kaffeyeh* and tough black robes over droopy slacks and logging boots turned up at the toes like fat pagodas. The tent was both outside and inside and faced the east and Mecca. With about twenty from our tour, I entered, tentative, a room twenty-by-forty that was alive in its own shadows. It smelled of dry oils and burnt wood and coffee just getting started. The long strips of goat hair that made the tent were woven, one new strip a year, by the wife whose tent it will always be. When dry, the goats' hair is porous, admits the wind to cool and clear; when wet, it closes like knit fingers to keep out the storm.

We sat on plump pillows as bright as the rugs that covered the ground. At an oak tree container in the center of the tent, the sheik squatted in his bright robe and ground coffee with a pestle in a thundering rhythm that told other tents "guests are here." Men offered us hospitality—steaming coffee said to be strong as gunpowder.

Then we women were invited to the women's quarters, always apart. "Notice carefully all of it," said Joseph, our guide, for even he, second-in-charge of Arab affairs in Israel, had not seen what is there. We went to the south end of the tent, out and around boys in pale, Western clothing playing about deserted jeeps, trucks, the rusting of everything. Here, as in most of Israel and the Russia I had seen, the never subtle preservation of old violence.

At the opening, the stout woman of the tent with a smile brown at the gums exudes a magnificent sense of domain. Grandly she welcomes our seeing her sand-shined pans hanging over a small fire that has never gone out, the swept earth, her elaborately embroidered robe. She hallows it, this protectorate of beautiful brown generations. Happily occupied, the women smile quickly, then return to themselves. One girl, a mother, diffidently proud, cuddles a huge-eyed baby with a goatskin pacifier shaped like a thumb.

We have heard that the sheik might be polygamous, so we try to ask which of the ten or twelve children scattered about belong to the woman. She understands the hovering of our words and gestures. Her thick braids doubled and hung with coins, swing with her bracelets of silver and heavy beads. She points as if in the gathering of grapes, to this one, that one. She lingers on a knobby boy of eight or nine, darkly wonderful, who ducks, grins, and runs behind some others to disappear.

She looks at us, back at him. Still pointing to where he is, she eloquently bares her brown breast and lays her brown hand over it. Stunned by the grace of the mother tongue, I hear her say, "We are women here."

Years later, grieving for the deaths in the Gulf War, then in Afghanistan, and now in Iraq and Afghanistan again, I remember her and imagine that boy grown into a soldier to perhaps be gunned down as an enemy of my country. Or maybe even as a suicide bomber? What for his mother? My prayer, then as now, is simple:

> Woman of the tent, let me bring home your dark eyes and the secret of their holiness. . . . Spin through me. Teach me the threads and belonging in endless distance to this tenderness, this human resurrection.

But the human resurrection was to be short-lived. Three wars would engulf my America and the world I thought I had come to know. Any anger we had been nibbling at now erupted in a whole new scenario.

On Friday after 9/11 came the day of memorials, of presidential edict to pray for faith and hope. In Washington, in the National Cathedral, the president and assembled dignitaries heard the "Battle Hymn of the Republic" and proclamations of rightness that could surely counter acts of evil. In Salt Lake City, in the new Conference Center, twenty thousand at a time heard two sessions of talks by the First Presidency and music, including the acclaimed rendition of the "Battle Hymn" by the Tabernacle Choir. Be patient. Hold to your faith. Trust in the Lord—televised to millions. The first number on the program was "Where Can I Turn for Peace?" by the choir. "When with a wounded heart, anger, or malice, / I draw myself apart, / Searching my soul?" Words I had written in personal despair those years before, when our daughter was desperately ill. Now, surprisingly, they resounded with an expansion greater than any private agony. For my country, for my people and others around the world—where to turn for peace?

Half an hour later, I was at a birthday lunch with seven of my oldest friends. We'd been pals since grade school, for more than seventy years. Two were in wheelchairs, one bent with osteoporosis, another with rheumatoid arthritis and a stroke; two of us had had minor strokes, and another, bouts with debilitating depression. But we would make the lunch no matter what.

We had been part of that "good war" Tom Brokaw described in his *The Greatest Generation*. Our husbands had served on carriers, in planes, in the invasion with General Eisenhower. Mel was overseas at nineteen helping to free Paris. Now we sat remembering and shaking our heads over a new kind of war. It was noon, time for the moment of silence to honor the dead, the injured, the heroic in New York and Washington. In a crowded restaurant, what for our table of old women? We were linked by three-quarters of a century of keeping homes as we kept our equanimity in capricious history, from the Great Depression to four distant wars, through recessions and deaths of enough loved ones that we were older than almost everyone. But we were there, caring about each other, our progeny, our intimate welfare, and our now broader-than-ever take on the world.

Without cue, we eight bowed our heads and took hold of hands, something we had never done in all our years of celebrations and trials. On one side, I felt Virginia, in a wheelchair from a broken hip and despondent over the recent death of her husband of fifty-two years; across from her, Joyce, in a wheelchair from post-polio syndrome. Both have since died. On my other hand, I felt Pat, on an hour's leave from duties as matron of a temple. I felt in their hands a pulsing of strength. No timid or forced flowing of self into self. For me, this circle raced with an energy usually evoked by intense well-being, from meditation or sensuous awareness.

None of us could know what even the next hour might bring, but in that moment of connecting to each other and to the God we all believed in, I was privy to a peace beyond understanding, what mystics seek and devotees hope for. The peace, that only moments before felt so bludgeoned by a whole new acquaintance with horror. A poem I wrote during the Gulf War about the birth of my eleventh grandson ended, "Grow, shine, keep being. And be anything but maybe . . . And to you, little boy: when you are / the weight of a man, do more than whimper / I am only one, there is nothing I can do. There is so much."

Was it all just grandma talk? I am still only one. In a world now shivering again—*my* world this time—I talk to my friends or to my senators in Washington: What to do? How to help? How ever to make even a minute difference? What comes to mind is that circle of very old friends, matriarchs all, leaning on our learned belief in restoration through prayer. How different from my bedouin woman in her tent or a Russian woman in her cemetery? And I remember a magic New Year's Eve when five hundred million of us around the world joined in just such a meditation for peace. I also remember being with three hundred delegates from twenty-three countries coming together to espouse a test ban treaty in Kazakhstan, only a border away from Afghanistan.

I think of the daring and dignity of my "peace friends" eager to remove minefields from paths of innocents in Cambodia or Afghanistan or take food and schools to the hungry and uneducated instead of bombs. Of course, I'm distressed about a first-strike war that has brought death and devastation and so little of the proposed good life in its wake. Yet I find solace in the good I know to be in those asking for patience and partners in their plans for scouring out terrorism. We need each other, and each other's strengths.

Even as I pray for safety and success for our troops abroad, I'll remember what the "Battle Hymn of the Republic" has to say to us at home. Written by a woman, Julia Ward Howe, during the Civil War, she declares, "Mine eyes have seen the glory of the coming of the Lord; / He is trampling out the vintage where the grapes of wrath are stored." What better than to trample out this season's yield of anger and malice—to be healed by whatever grounds us in hope and love? No, I will not let invaders of our financial and military strongholds have access to my strongholds of faith and caring. I must find ways still to nibble away at whatever anger there is in the world.

And blazing in my mind will stay the impromptu prayer of President Gordon B. Hinckley in the closing session of the Mormon semiannual conference on Sunday, October 7, 2001. He had earlier said, "I have just been handed a note. It says a U.S. missile attack is underway [in Afghanistan]. I need not remind you that we live in perilous times." An impatient, inflamed 90 percent of the nation approved the bombing to begin rooting out the terrorists. But there had to be more than bombing.

Articulate as well as compassionate at ninety-one, he ended his talk:

> Now we are at war. Great forces are being mobilized. Political alliances are being forged. We do not know how long this conflict will last. We do not know what it will cost in lives and treasure. . . . Let us not panic nor go to extremes. Let us be prudent in every respect. And above all, let us move forward with faith in the living God and his beloved Son.

Then, without precedent of any president in more than a century and a half of Mormon general conferences, his spontaneous prayer:

> Bless the cause of peace and bring it quickly to us again. We humbly plead with thee asking that thou will forgive our arrogance, pass by our sins, be kind and gracious to us and cause our hearts to turn with love to thee.

In an invocation at a luncheon the next day for the graduate school of social work at the University of Utah, one of my best "peace friends," Dee Rowland, government liaison of the Salt Lake Catholic diocese, said:

Let us pray for those who are powerful and those who are powerless. Let us pray for those who are hopeless without power and those who are with power but without conscience. Let us pray for all those who lie under bombs and for those who dispatch them and for those who make them. Let us pray for the innocent, the firefighters, the police, and the rescue workers, for the villagers halfway around the globe, and for the soldiers, and for those who go to kill and are killed. Let us pray for all who believe and yet do not hope. Let us pray for all those who hope and yet do not live out their hope. Let us pray for ourselves and for all we love and for all, finally, who await our love.

And for any suffering this war will cause and has already caused. As Jeanette Rankin has said, "No one can win a war any more than anyone can win an earthquake." The earthquake continues these years after the war in Iraq has been declared over. Nothing could have brought that reality closer than a visit in November 2003, with a thirty-three-year-old captain of the 1457th Engineer Battalion home on two-week leave from duty in Iraq. He would become a face in the war across the globe.

He called me from Arizona, where he was home to be with his wife and two young daughters and to see for the first time his five-month-old son. After earning his degree in engineering, he had gone to Harvard for his MBA and started a dream job near Phoenix. Three days later, he was called up to head his group of nearly two hundred Utahns headed for Iraq in November 2002. Their primary job—locating and dismantling land mines.

Mines [he told me] are the perfect soldiers—always on duty, never any worry about morale, just right there to blow to bits any unwary man, woman, or child who might cross a street or head for a field.

I thought of Mel's dearest friend, Wilbur Braithwaite, nearly sixty years after his WWII encounter with a mine in France. Miraculously, his wounded legs sufficiently healed for him to play basketball and coach tennis. But a thirteenth surgery in recent years on his nose still could not stop the hemorrhages that sent him from Manti, Utah, three hours to the emergency room in Salt Lake every few months.

Now my young friend tells me of leading his battalion on high-profile missions. Called the "911 unit," in an emergency, they are the first responders. In addition to dismantling mines, they have helped reopen the airport, critical bridges, and even the zoo. They have built a marketplace in conjunction with Iraqis in Baghdad to replace a market that sold only weapons, where shooting was as common as exchange. Then he was telling of his convoy of five Humvees headed for the Kirzah International Airport outside of Baghdad, where they had been clearing up. About a third of the way there, the lead vehicle just ahead of his disappeared in a ball of fire. A bomb was planted against a cement pylon. This young father (to me still a boy), whom I'd seen grow up, was in charge of digging through the rubble, finding bodies, even looking for an eyeball of a buddy whose face was gone and for fingers—"digits" he called them—of two other survivors with split abdomens who were sent off with medics from his unit.

The day before we talked, the number of American deaths since "victory" had been declared had far surpassed the 115 killed in combat before the announcement. Regular army personnel were going home after a year there. Men like him in the Reserve or National Guard had just been told their service was extended to a year and a half and could be extended over and over again. He was headed back the next day.

"So how do you feel about being there?" I asked.

Nobody wants to be there. People are getting along, doing a job. Can't do anything about getting out sooner. People still thank us—mostly poor people. The 10 percent who were wealthy under Saddam are leading the resistance. We have to keep telling ourselves that the only things worse than war are the reasons that drive people to war.

His loyalty to a cause almost obscured the bleakness in his voice.

We've taken on an ominous responsibility. We can't ransack and then desert. We need to see it through—the only thing worse than invading is to leave those people subject to rebel governments. I wish Bush would be more humble, get some help. Iraq would welcome Mideastern support more than anything from the West. They don't trust Christians. They want the U.S. out, others in. As long as we're there, attacks will never stop. Too much bad blood.

Nearly forty-five minutes later, newly informed and with a sadness I'd not known so immediately in this wartime, I asked, "And what can we do, we folks back here, to support you?"

"We've learned from mistakes in Vietnam. To give total support for troops, there needs to be a human face to war."

I had my human face. The picture of him in his dark crew cut and army fatigues, standing amidst two thousand soldiers in his batallion, would stay with me. For a long time, he will be waving good-bye again, holding to his five-month-old baby and hugging his wife and little daughters. And then back in that Humvee, approaching overpasses and digging through rubble for bodies.

"But how do I show my support?"

"Be for or against. Be politically active—voice opinions either way. Just don't be passive."

I thought back to my poem to my eleventh grandson—"Be anything but maybe."

Soldiers resent not caring—forgetting. Now, instead of faces of the dead or interviews with their families in the media, there are only minor headlines—Two SOLDIERS KILLED IN BAGHDAD. Write your congressmen; say you want the reserves home! Tell them we're people over there.

Then I remembered visiting Ground Zero in New York, the gaping hole waiting for new buildings, but even more the venerable St. Paul's Chapel, part of lower Manhattan for 235 years. Only a block away from the attack on September 11, even its windows were miraculously unshattered in the blast and collapsing of the towers. There, hundreds of workers found refuge, the benches where they slept still bear gashes from their belts and boots (now regarded as "sacramental marks"). Exhausted psyches and bodies were comforted there by volunteers and prayers of every faith. Workers found buckets of candy and lip balm, had massages and foot baths dried by hands that assuaged the damage of hot ashes, and teddy bears cozied into their arms as they sat dazed from fourteen-hour duty in rubble not unlike what my young captain and his battalion of Utahns were searching in—both looking for victims of violence to spirits as much as to bodies.

I remembered being on top of the Empire State Building in New York, looking down at bug-sized police cars—sixteen of them converging to control the crowd assembling for blocks. "Why?" I ask a stranger next to me.

"A protesters' parade," he points out.

"But why? The war has started. Lots of us protested every way we knew how before last week. But what's the point now?"

His answer fits my young captain's exactly. "Look at me. I was in Vietnam for five years. I'd still be there if it hadn't been for protesters." If not for people being more than anguished at the reality of war.

The reality of war—in the Union Building at the University of Utah, on Armistice (Veterans) Day, November 11, 2003, students hung a black paper chain like we used to make of red and green for

Christmas. Nothing could have prepared me for the sight—strung across the two-story ceilings, up and down columns, over walls and windows, the black reminder. Down one broad hall, students bent over studies or slouched in overstuffed chairs, on break from classes. Next to them, high windows reflected the prayed-for snow on still-leafed trees after long drought—relief. In lowercase, "theater," at the far end hung high between wide scallops of the black chain. A red poster in the front foyer—CHAIN OF REMEMBRANCE. EACH ONE OF THESE LINKS REPRESENTS AN INDIVIDUAL WHO HAS DIED AS A RESULT OF WAR SINCE SEPTEMBER 11, 2001. (ON THIS DAY, SEVENTEEN THOUSAND LINKS.) SOLDIERS, CIVILIANS, IRAQIS, JOURNALISTS/ REPORTERS, ALL PART OF THE CONFLICT. ONE HUMAN FAMILY. How many since then?

Here in the baffling conundrums of politics and power, we can offer sustenance of heart and means. I can do more than grieve over death and destruction. I can love my country by caring enough to keep informed, listen to others, and express my views. I will refuse to be lied to. I will be politically informed. I will vote. Even as I can hold hands and pray with old friends or for a newly found buddy on his way back to Baghdad.

From his last e-mail:

I just feel tired. . . . I have been affected by what I have seen here. It has made me deeply grateful for so much that I took for granted. It has also somewhat disheartened me on man's inhumanity to man. Some of what I have seen first-hand has shocked and dismayed me how we can treat each other the way we do. So much violence is done in the name of God and religion but if you look really at the root of major religions they all teach peace and coexistence. I don't understand how we could go so wrong.

Of course, I will anguish over hurt in the world or in those I love. And sometimes I will lose heart over that anguish. But even in my anger at my young friend's having to make war in battles beyond my understanding, I believe that God does answer privately our own reaching, anybody's reaching for solace and direction. To help anything go better, I can hold to my faith that prayers do matter whether in cathedrals or conference centers, synagogues or places of meditation, in a far desert or with children by a bedside. I can turn for peace every hour of every day or night and be assured that God will answer privately, reach my reaching, anybody's reaching. And reach to others on either side of battles way beyond my understanding.

I will stay involved. I will cling to my hopes as well as my concerns. Sometimes I will have the chance to express my joy in observing peace on this beloved earth:

4/10/05
To the Editors of the *Deseret Morning News* and the *Salt Lake Tribune*

Imagine! It is possible! For three days millions of people milling about in intimate proximity without an untoward incident. Catholics, Jews, Muslims, Eastern Orthodox, Protestants, Evangelicals, Mormons, Anglicans, Buddhists, Hindus, etc., etc., believers and nonbelievers—faiths and nationalities with uncommon history and inclination, all gathered in common reverence. In peace. And in recognition of the many kinds of goodness there are in the world. Thousands even stood in line together for twenty-four hours without altercation or protest! What dreamer could have conceived such an assemblage? What head of state, what leader of an ideology, of a people, of a generation? What science fiction writer? And beyond that assemblage, way past a billion of us glued to TV and what was taking place in that for three-days-holy space?

Yes, this was a world made whole, a congregation of human beings being the best they know how to be, for that brief time allied in the wonder of what one good man had reaped in his travels to their countries and hearts. For once no need to argue issues, "one and onlys," no railing against difference, or posturing for attention. Solemnity held sway in a joyful acknowledgment of greatness. Pope John Paul II, you must have been smiling that for once we so often irreverent, volatile, opinionated, and unthoughtful human beings felt and actually came together in loving-kindness. Thank you for teaching us how.

Only by working on the weather of peace can we expect to nibble away at the burgeoning anger in the world. It has to begin with me.

| CHAPTER 7 |

THE STATIONS OF THE CROSS

Pure resonance with suffering can recognize that human beings of whatever culture are not intrinsically different. Once experienced, it will alter everything from then on.
—John Howard Griffith

Whatever draws one person to another as a friend has much more to do with the human spirit than with age, station, color, or background—and certainly a lot less to do with religious affiliation than with the impulse to lift and honor that spirit in one another. A mutual response to beauty and believing can bring together what might seem very unlikely companions. Involvement in joy or suffering—or even a committee with a common cause—can do even more.

In April 1983, three years before my accident, I met Paul Fini, a young painter from Chicago, at the Virginia Center for the Creative Arts. The resonance of his life in mine would come years later after he had died of AIDS. That first chilly morning at VCCA, while walking to my studio, I came across Paul leaning over the fence feeding his apple core to Sugar Daddy. Paul, a runner, was wearing shorts.

"Aren't you freezing?" I asked, rubbing the gelding's nose.

"No. Not really. I need to use my body when I paint."

"And what are you painting that takes that kind of input?"

"The fourteen stations of the cross," he said, referring to the events between Christ's sentencing and his burial. "I have to hurry," he added. "I promised to have them done by Easter—for a friend in New York. He died last month of AIDS." AIDS. In 1983, that was a new word to me and I had no idea what it might mean. I mentioned to Paul that I had just finished a book of poems and journal entries, *Once in Israel*, in which I'd written about the stations of the cross, which I'd seen in Jerusalem.

It turned out that I had to return home to Utah the day I met Paul because of a daughter's illness. When I returned to VCCA, Paul met me at the door. He said he'd found *Once in Israel* in the library, cried as he read it, and had identified with every word.

I remembered my own profound encounter with Israel a few years previously. I remembered the afternoon on the Via Dolorosa, following the path of Jesus on his last day, how the hymn I'd learned as a child, "I Walked Today Where Jesus Walked," seemed suddenly a hopelessly sanitized evocation of that dusty street, of the stops a doomed man had had to make.

I. The Condemnation by Pilate

II. Reception of the Cross

III. Christ's First Fall

IV. Meeting with his Mother

V. Simon of Cyrene Carries the Cross

VI. Veronica Wipes the Face of Christ

VII. The Second Fall

VIII. Christ's Exhortation to the Women of Jerusalem

IX. The Third Fall

X. Stripping of the Clothes

XI. Jesus Is Nailed to the Cross

XII. The Death

XIII. Descent from the Cross
XIV. The Burial

What about Paul's paintings of the stations? Could I see them? He had finished them, and they had hung in the VCCA Gallery—a one-day exhibit only on Easter.

Before I even unpacked, he took me to his room, pulled the paintings one at a time from under his bed where, large as they were—three by four feet—they could lie flat. I couldn't have imagined or anticipated them, so unlike any depiction I had seen. I was overcome by the pure emotion on the canvas. Pain, torment, and radiance—indeed an apt memorial for his friend. The only color—shades of blood red. The paintings raced in my head, lifted me past the small room to an acquaintance with suffering that was totally new. I was profoundly moved, as if I knew Christ and his message for the first time.

I asked if I could take Paul's picture with any painting he chose. He agreed, but with a half smile that I remembered two weeks later when I called him in Chicago. "The photo didn't turn out," I said. "The only shot on the whole roll that didn't."

Over the phone, I sensed that same smile. "I knew it wouldn't," he said. Years later, I would have professional slides made of the paintings—twice. They wouldn't turn out either.

I had glimpsed Paul's sense of the religious in the slides of his work he presented at VCCA, showing icons, miniatures, studies of El Greco saints. We talked religion: his Catholicism, my Mormonism, his master's thesis work done in Haiti, my trip to Israel, my balancing act as teacher, writer, tennis instructor, friend, wife, and mother of five.

Then, early in my stay, Paul asked to do a tarot reading for me—another step into territory I had before viewed as superstition. But other residents told me I was lucky, that Paul was selective in volunteering readings, and very gifted. Only a month before, they said, Paul had joined an astrologer, a palmist, and a handwriting expert in performing a "human installation" (a work of art not painting or sculpture) at the Chicago Art Institute, where he'd received his Master of Fine Arts degree. Patrons had lined up for a block waiting, and Paul had given eighty readings in a day. I was curious. And I trusted Paul.

Paul dealt the cards. I selected and asked the questions—and was dumbfounded by his answers. For example, when I asked about each daughter, he said about one, "She's frantic. Call her at once." I protested that this daughter was particularly fine. But when the reading ended, I phoned, and her first words were, "Mother, I'm so glad you called. This has been the most frantic week of my life."

I asked about my work and Paul told me my writing would begin to go well on the eighth day. I no more counted days than clouds, but on the eighth my typewriter clattered into action.

"On your way home be careful of an extremity," he warned. Carrying a heavy suitcase through the airport, I felt my shoulder give. Pain. Emergency surgery would be required to remove staples put in two years earlier following a skiing accident.

Paul Fini—a wonder? In every way. He was dark and handsome, with a cropped beard and the slimness of a runner. His bearing and smile, though, were reminiscent of Pavarotti's as he enlisted a chef's crew of residents to create a master fettuccine dinner or viewed the surrounding beauty of the Blue Ridge Mountains. And he painted incessantly, prolifically.

During the next two years, we ended up in the same artists' colony three more times. For part of those two years, he had been part-time cook at Ragdale, a retreat in Lake Forest, just outside Chicago, and he urged me to come for a month to the prairie to write. A city boy, he was enthralled with the prairie—tiny new frogs leaping out of our reflections as we lay on our stomachs drinking from a hidden spring that bubbled out of the bronze of fields in fall. "This is real," he told me. "Like what I base my life on—the rock—religion, God in all of it."

One day over lunch on the grass just outside my studio at VCCA, Paul had said, "I always thought that my work—painting—was the most important thing for me. But now I know that loving one person and having it two-way is by far the most significant thing in my life." He liked hearing about my husband of thirty-four years; sometimes he brought David to visit, knowing I would like him. Coming from my traditional Mormon culture, I might have expected to be uncomfortable around them. I was anything but. We all became pals.

———

Gradually, starting in 1984, I became increasingly aware that Paul was not well. Never, however, did he suggest that he might have AIDS. He continued being optimistic, ably filling his time with painting and with David. He sent me postcards—one a golden Madonna with a manger scene in her crown. On the back, "The heart is the toughest part of the body. Tenderness is in the hands" —Carolyn Forche. He signed, "XXXX Paul."

In January 1985, a call came not from Paul but from David. Paul had had surgery and been in intensive care for two days. He had lymphoma, well advanced. Only then did I learn how sick Paul had been. I told my journal:

Since summer, stomach pains, diarrhea, bleeding, pale. Had been in the hospital all last week for tests. Couldn't be diagnosed without surgery. CT scan alarming—a mass. An aggressive tumor in the small intestine. He'll have to have chemo.

[Then from my journal on March 25:] Paul is better! Called tonight, talked for much more than the scant three or so minutes last week. Even laughed. Fever down, still on strong IV antibiotics, but sounded so much stronger. Oh, am I glad. Whole evening changed.

The battle raged all year, and by October, David was telling me how the cancer had filled Paul, bloating his insides, taking over his spine, obliterating his head and spirit—yet never a word about AIDS. Every time I had talked to Paul, he said, "I'm going to be okay, Emma Lou." His last postcard to me ended with, "I hope to be back to Ragdale in the winter to paint."

Then on a Sunday night a few months later, I turned Paul's card up on my Rolodex, ready to call the hospital. I was going to be in Chicago the following week, and I planned to surprise Paul with a visit. But David was on the line when I picked up the phone. "I was just going to call you," I said.

David answered, "Paul said, 'Emma Lou will call.'"

"I'm coming to Chicago on Thursday," I said. "Shall I come right now?"

"He won't know you. He's in a coma. But he wants you to have the paintings, the stations of the cross. He said that over and over."

I knew. He had told me before.

I missed Paul's memorial by one day, held in St. Sebastian's Church. He was thirty-four, the age of my oldest daughter. My sixty-first birthday was the day before, reminding me of his gift to me the year we met. The small, ancient silver box embossed with a rose still sat on the dresser in our home; he had inscribed, "Happy birthday 1983, Emma Lou, with mucho love, Paul." Again from my journal:

October 28: David met my plane, took me to the big blue Victorian house. . . . Paul's studio spread with canvas over hard wood, four paintings, oils, brushes neat on a table, wonderful sight. Hard to see, but so glad I did. David's map of rivers on his wall. . . . David and I both had trouble when he handed me the printed program of the memorial I missed.

On one page, from poet Philip Brooks, Episcopal bishop:

Do not pray for an easy life,
Pray to be a stronger person.

Do not pray for tasks equal to your powers,
    Pray for powers equal to your tasks.
Then the doing of your work shall be no miracle,
    But YOU shall be a miracle.

Also, David opened the *Chicago Tribune* from the Sunday before, when Paul was in the coma. A centerfold spread was headlined: HIGH-RISE ARTISTRY WITH AN ITALIAN ACCENT. And below, THREE LARGE PAINTINGS BY CHICAGO ARTIST PAUL FINI.

"I tried to tell him, to show him," David said. "It would have made him real happy."

He showed me where the stations still lay under the bed. "I'll box them and ship them to you as soon as I can let them go," he said. "I'll have to keep most of this pretty much the same, at least for now."

The following summer, I had my accident and death experience. David and I kept in touch. The summer of 1988, his bad news came. David had been diagnosed with Pneumocystis carinii pneumonia, most often associated with AIDS. He tried to reassure himself as well as me in his letter:

> Emma Lou, all I can say is, right now I look and feel the best that I have in a long time. . . . I am not frightened. . . . I think that I am going to be around for a while yet. . . . My friends are being very supportive. I've joined a support group that works with healing and living (and not dying).

We talked often about faith, and I grappled with telling him about my death experience, still too timid to accept the full implication of my return to teach what had been shown to me.

In his support group, he reported later, he asked himself, "What does the Lord want me to do?" His answer to himself, "Be encouraging to people who have AIDS." David sought spiritual strength in the gospel singing he loved. He also had insurance, an attentive doctor, and aggressive medical treatment. Nevertheless, month by month, his condition worsened.

As 1990 began, he wrote:

> I'm not feeling as well as I once did. I have to do anything
> I have to do in the morning. I feel like being with people,
> but they don't come around any more. Everyone hates to see
> people deteriorate. . . . Six to twelve friends—not all close—
> have died. People now are afraid of me—even to drive me
> home. No one can ever talk about the real thing.

We talked in superficial ways that I was to regret. What about his lifestyle? How? Why? What agonies or ecstasies for him? Only about the dread disease.

By May, he called to say he had spent a month in Florida with his parents, felt good though still tired, and looked forward to trying a new medicine. He said he had mustered the courage to send me the paintings. Very few people had seen them after the Easter exhibition.

The stations arrived, rolled and mailed in a tall box. I unpacked them on our king-size bed and looked at them one at a time. The same awe. What in the world would I do with them?

David's AIDS now took a deadly grip on him. His mother came to Chicago to care for him as his pain and confusion intensified. Paul's parents came to visit. On October 14, David told me on the phone:

> I feel okay, but I lost my mother a couple of days ago. She
> had not been sick but she fainted in the hall, and died before
> the paramedics got here—of a ruptured aorta. She's taken
> care of me and everything for the past six months.

He sounded empty. Emotion seemed to have deserted him like so much else. He would go to Florida with his father. He wanted to send me more of Paul's paintings but didn't have the strength.

By Christmas, David was in the hospital with pneumonia, delirious, thinking he was on the river. His brother closed down the Chicago apartment and sent Paul's paintings to a secondhand store. Finally, down to one hundred pounds, David died in a nursing home. No memorial for now, his father said. Later, he might send his remains to Chicago to his mother's grave.

What kind of rejection and condemnation had David lived with? How could I tell of his value, of what I knew him to be? What kind of cowardice kept me from writing about him or Paul? Who in my culture could ever understand my affection for them? Had my accident prepared me to speak for both when many I also loved would call them "not our kind of people"?

David was gone. Paul's other paintings were gone.

Yet, standing beside my bed, rolled up in the tall box, fourteen paintings pulsed with blood and light. Somewhere they had to be hung and seen in sequence, all of them visible at once, their power incremental from one to the next.

Why left to me? I wondered.

But then, I knew—to be a bridge between Paul's world and mine. To be seen as a vehicle for understanding—not only the paintings and the stations, their significance, but the painter and his significance. Significance of the pain and the loss of a Paul or a David. And the impetus to contribute to what might have saved one or both.

As time passed, I recalled the most puzzling thing Paul had predicted during that tarot reading when we were hardly acquainted. "You and I are going to do something together, Emma Lou. Maybe you'll write words for my paintings."

And so, out of the night and into the wonder that moved and compelled him, I did, both story and poem. And waited to see where Paul and his paintings would find their way.

PAUL FINI'S STATIONS OF THE CROSS, ALL IN THE COLOR OF BLOOD

Look.
The red is the stillness of unfinished action,
the white the spaces that widen and close.

Who can turn away
from the turning of canvas and color
charged to include us?

What happened, happens
in fourteen groundings we
cannot escape.
Nothing moves without
our permission. Everything
stays without being asked.

In its absence,
the figure is origin and reason,
present, a presence

in the quiet of unquiet stirrings
that hide any wound
from beginning to no end.

In the summer of 1992, Merline Leaming called. I knew her best as a distinguished interior designer, someone I'd consulted for decades about furnishings that would outlast both fads and the wear of a household of seven. Now she said, "I want to take you to lunch with Gary Collins next week. I think you'd like each other." I was surprised but intrigued. Of course, I wanted to meet Gary. One of his paintings livened the jacket of my last book of poems, *Things Happen*, yet I'd met him only briefly. Merline was right—we all liked each other, a lot.

We talked art, and during dessert, I found myself telling the story of Paul and his paintings. They were fascinated, wanted to see them. Late in September, we found an afternoon. At home in my home, Merline and Gary asked about every photograph and memento, and it took an hour to reach the bedroom where Paul's paintings had lived for more than two years. I laid each on the bed, one at a time. The light was bad, for it was now dusk, but the paintings held their own illumination. Gary and Merline brought practiced eyes to what I had seen but not seen, and they exulted.

Before they left, late for other appointments, we were partners in a venture that would take the paintings from my bedroom to the world on a journey none of us then envisioned. I gave them copies of the story I'd written of the paintings. They wanted time to think.

They brought friends to the next meeting. Gary talked about framing and display. Merline had me read them my story of the paintings. Ray Kingston, renowned architect and recent member of the National Endowment for the Arts, admitted later he had come expecting the Emperor's New Clothes. He had seen too much emotion flung on canvas, trying to pass for art. He was happily surprised at what he saw. By our next meeting, Ray had ideas for the paintings to travel—to be exhibited nationwide.

Meanwhile, I talked with medical people familiar with AIDS. One contacted Greg Pedroza, ecumenical advisor for Catholic parishes, who came to our next meeting. He had an undergraduate degree in fine arts and a master's in theology. He told us later he had left St. Vincent's Church, saying, "I'll be about half an hour. Some lady has some stations she wants me to see."

As I laid the paintings on the bed, awestruck, Greg explained what had mystified the rest of us—a cross here, a grid there, lines, margins, thickness of color. By coincidence, his parish had been explicating the stations of the cross for Lent. Just that week, Greg had written about them.

As the others gathered, Greg continued to talk. His church

just happened to have an adjoining hall where fourteen very large paintings could be displayed. He would talk to the Father in charge. Our next meeting would be at St. Vincent's.

The following week, Greg called me to say that his cousin, one of a part-Catholic, part-Mormon family in Orem, had died of AIDS. The family had opted to list the cause of death in his obituary—a rare choice at that time. From all over Utah County came calls thanking them for their courage.

"We've lived with this secret."

"What a brave thing to do for all of us."

The young man who died was a great-great-grandson of Wilford Woodruff, fourth president of the Mormon Church. Greg said that his extended family wanted to finance the framing of the paintings—all of them.

For our first meeting at St. Vincent's, we unrolled and spread out the paintings on the floor, seen all together for the first time since Easter, a decade earlier. Even I had never seen them except one at a time. Again, awe. A whole new experience. But how to display them? Ideas flowed. A month of meetings later, we watched Ray, the architect, sketch a prospective exhibit. Three weeks after that, his drawing of easels, on which each painting would hang, had been translated into wooden crosses by his friend Richard Fetzer, master cabinetmaker.

My good friend June Nebeker, teacher of art history, met with us as the group evolved and she contributed ideas for flowers, music, and understatement. Kelly Chopis and Robert Austin of the AIDS Foundation were astounded at our donating the paintings to the foundation and discussed having them accompany the AIDS quilt for display across the country.

Wondering how to light the paintings in the huge vaulted hall with fluorescent ceiling lights, we eventually placed votive candles at the base of each painting as it hung on its cross—no one's suggestion or decision, yet everyone's. A thousand invitations were mailed to our separate constituencies. My grandmother's cut-glass punch bowl would accept donations to the AIDS Foundation.

Advertising executive Skip Branch joined us, offered to handle media coverage, and made brochures for participants to take home.

Paul's birthday was February 13, and as the day approached, I wrote his parents about the planned exhibit. We had not been in touch since Paul's death. Paul's father wrote me:

> My wife and I were delighted to receive your most welcome letter of Feb. 7, which is my seventy-fourth birthday. We were even more pleased that you still remember our son Paul and also his birthday. Paul is always on our mind and we were especially happy to know that others also think of him. We are also very grateful that you will hang some of Paul's paintings in the hopes of inspiring others in a very worthwhile cause. . . . On June 15, 1991, we celebrated our fiftieth wedding anniversary. . . . We had a great time with our family and friends but Paul was dearly missed. In fact David was also missed.

The next day, a letter from Paul's mother came, who, her husband had written, was suffering from cancer and diabetes, and recovering from heart surgery:

> Dear Emma Lou, My angel husband has filled you in on illness (mine); I thank God not his. . . . I am most grateful for each day; but more grateful for the love and care he surrounds me with. . . . Thank you for your kindness to Paul, Emma Lou, my heart and soul still scream in pain over our loss of him.

The exhibit fell on the last day of Passover, the day after Easter, a Monday. On Sunday, in my Mormon ward, I resounded with the truth, "He is risen." Monday evening, I felt again elevated in a spacious Catholic church, this time by an overflow gathering representing many faiths. Surely, I thought, before me sits what Christ intended when he said, "Love one another as I have loved you." I thought of the generosity, the combining of talents and time, and the whole joyous process that placed Paul Fini's paintings on display in the City of the Saints.

"Paul," I mentally telegraphed, "your paintings, and you, have found a home."

It was not to be the end of our association.

———

For years, the pastor of the First Baptist Church, a friend and neighbor, had asked me to represent the Mormon faith on the Baptists' heralded Christmas program. Leaders of various faiths, all but me wearing clerical attire, marched in procession to read scripture between tender and powerful renderings by the Salt Lake Symphonic Choir.

Nearly a year later, the same huge chapel and balcony were filled with a different audience. It was World AIDS Day. Again I had been asked to speak, but I had urged Mormon leaders to send an official emissary; they had urged me to go, unofficial as always. I was uncertain and invited the night to help me know what to do. By morning, I felt from my reliable mystic informing that I should be there.

But Mormon services are relatively unadorned, and I did not anticipate the offerings of the various clergy at this service. After a men's choir sang, we were to surround the altar behind the pulpit to place and explain a symbol of our faith in healing.

I was nervous enough to be only vaguely aware of what others placed on the altar—a chalice, a Bible, vials of oil, written ceremonies. I clutched my mother's tiny brass pillbox that I had pulled from my purse, now a makeshift substitute for a small bottle of oil. I announced:

In our church, two men holding the priesthood lay their hands on the head of whoever is receiving the blessing. One anoints that head with the consecrated oil, and the other pronounces a very personalized prayer to invoke healing.

After we placed our offerings, the pastor asked members of the audience to say aloud the name of someone they particularly wished to be healed. The vaulted chapel echoed with names. My husband and daughter told me later they both said, "Paul Fini," though Paul had been dead for more than eight years.

After we sat, a young woman gave a moving account of her contracting and living with HIV and then AIDS. More singing by the choir, and it was my turn to speak. From the pulpit, I could feel the heartbeat of that rapt crowd as I told the story of Paul, the paintings, and the exhibit. I ended with, "Tonight is like that night—a time of helping others to understand not only the paintings, but the painter, and to help assuage the pain so alive in both."

The program ended. I started to make my way up the aisle to meet my family only to find a line of participants wanting to talk to me. A returned missionary from eastern Utah, with tears in his eyes: "Thank you for bringing some Mormonism to me. It's been such a long time." A young woman I'd known through tennis with her parents: "You reminded me of my grandmother when you spoke. This is my friend, my partner." An older man who had sung in the choir: "My old life as a high school teacher ended when I . . ." He hesitated, knowing my daughters were some he had taught. "But I really appreciated your being here tonight," he added. "It felt good to see someone from that life."

It took nearly half an hour to talk to those waiting to tell me, never without emotion, the same story. They felt marginalized, defined out of so much in the Mormonism they still loved. Difference did the defining. They warmed to the comfort of a healing, if only for one night, through the joining of faiths and faith and caring for each other.

"The two great commandments in action," I thought, "to love God and the neighbor sitting down the row."

OUTSIDE MY HISTORY

Outsiders they seem,
these strong, fragile ones.

They stay their distance.

Until one day you stumble inside their history
and find you are human.

One time is all it takes
to meet one, any one outside your landscape.

There, coming to know that one,
you know you are mortal too,

that to be part of their ordeal,
to kneel beside them at any distance,
is to whisper to both of you,

it is not too late.
I would love you.
I would touch your history with what I have to give.
As you have touched mine through yours.

With the privilege of a matriarch, I had once again been opened to possibility through exposure to the world, to the quality of people unlike me. Without any knowable intention, I had been a party to forgiveness, to understanding, and to offering what I never could have imagined without the grace that my accident had opened me up to. All I could think was "thank you."

CHAPTER 8

HEALERS

May healing be near to our hurt!
　　　　　　　—Eoghan Ruadh Mac an Bhaird

————————

Mystic might seem applicable only to the spiritual, but for me it has applied all my life to the physical as well. My heritage has taught five generations of my family reverence for the body. Through my family, I have grown up with the absolute love of movement and expectation of cures after any physical impairment. At nine, one of my brothers had a yearlong bout with osteomyelitis, an infection of the bone. In a day before antibiotics, the infection had destroyed his hip. In a new operation, skilled doctors fused it solid but predicted he might never walk again. Through prayer and loving encouragement, together with dedicated exercises (and a lot of cod liver oil), my father and mother helped him not only to walk but to have the ability to win a tennis tournament the summer after his seven months on crutches. Healing was as expected as spring after winter, as was help in the healing.

Before my accident, any rescue for me was through prayer and

Western medicine. Since my accident, cures have also come through complementary professionals.

———————

"Not again! It's 2:13 in the morning." My worried husband had reason to worry. "But hon, it's there. I've tried to ignore it and just go back to sleep, but it gets too awful. And then the labor pains . . ." Since the sixth month of this pregnancy, the gallbladder attacks, fierce and demanding. No curling up, no straightening out for relief, just more and more intense pain. No letting up, as in labor. No working it out like with the worst leg cramp. No aspirin to ease the pain. Most of all—no ignoring it. Especially when labor pains begin somewhere under and in back of it demanding, "Do something! Anything, but stop the pain. You can't have this baby this early."

Night after night, I'd fought the pain, had prayed for relief. We wanted this baby, our fifth. In 1962, there would have been no hope for the baby's survival at six months. The medical world had not yet learned how to save babies so early, certainly not when there was required surgery for the mother. Only a shot of IV Demerol, given to calm the gallbladder attack and let the labor pains stop, had worked. But what price the shots? Europe was producing deformed babies from a drug given mothers as a tranquilizer—Thalidomide babies with no arms or misshapen heads. But better to chance that than a dead baby?

My first gallbladder attack had started in the seventh month of my second pregnancy—only once, calmed by one shot of morphine in the emergency room. Then, with my next two pregnancies came more attacks, closer together but not more than four or five in all, only to disappear with delivery. During these pregnancies, Demerol calmed the pain and the babies made it to term. In the joy of having them, I forgot the problem, just as I did the throes of labor in a day when an epidural was unheard of. I adhered to my own maxim: nothing is hard that has a visible end. And labor did. An end full of surprise, too, since we never knew what sex the baby would be. After four girls, when people said to Mel, "Too bad you didn't get your boy," he answered in all honesty, "I could never love a boy like I do those girls."

But with this final baby, how to avoid the shots in the later weeks, sometimes two a night, with either my careful obstetrician or my doctor brother coming at any hour to bring that needle and relief? By the eighth month, I knew I was addicted. Teeth gritted in pain, I'd wage war with myself. Was it really this bad? Or was I simply a wimp, needing the 100 milligrams of IV drug?

At first, along with the relief, some euphoria smoothed me into the pillow. I loved everyone around, didn't care if I ever got out of bed, just so I could lie there floating at some distance that denied any need to move. But gradually, the relief turned into a miasma of unreality. Sleep, my forever friend, deserted me. I hung at the edge of some blur that never became sleep, woke with a cotton mouth and exhausted body. Eating was as much a chore as it had always been a pleasure. A gallbladder diet meant no meat, nothing with fat, my only dessert a piece of white toast in pear juice, after the canned pear.

I didn't want to see anyone, not even my husband, children, mother, or the good friends who tried to cheer or even talk to me. If anyone bumped the bed, I moaned in distress. I didn't read; I didn't want to. I didn't care about anything going on beyond that bleak bedroom. I tried to stay as motionless as possible for fear of triggering an attack. Some nights, I'd fight the pain and try to resist a shot until, not wanting to wake Mel, I'd go to my mother's bed in the other part of the house for strength to resist. But invariably, the labor pains would drive me to dial for help.

Of course, my doctors were only trying to get my baby here in a day when we women were taking Compazine for nausea and aspirin for pain, both of which, in years to come, would prove damaging to a fetus. Blessings by Mel or my brothers calmed me only temporarily, until one Saturday night two weeks before I was to deliver. A week before that, when the doctor thought it safe, I had gone to the hospital to be induced. Pitocin started labor and with it, grotesque gallbladder pain. Demerol shut down both, and I was sent home, despairing, to wait. After a blessing by Mel and a brother, labor started on its own—without any other pain. My baby was born in five quick hours, my shortest labor. Happy beyond expression, I saw that perfect little girl, beautiful, whole, blinking at her new world. And any desire for Demerol was gone.

But three days later, I was to have surgery for a tubal ligation, my ovarian tubes tied. It was too risky, I'd been convinced by the doctors, to have more children. We'd get our boys by the bounty of those gorgeous girls who would be more than fun to grow up with. But a tubal? Even though I had five children, it was not exactly part of what I'd ever wanted, let alone expected. In the night, awake to anguished misgivings, I looked up to see a nurse in her white cap and white uniform. She took my hand and quietly said:

Mrs. Thayne, I know how hard it is for you to decide to do this. But I promise you'll be glad—and so will your husband. I had a tubal ten years ago to save my health, and we've never had a better love life or life in all ways.

A stranger smiling at me. She held my hand and we talked for about an hour, time I'm sure she didn't have to give. But she was a woman about her business of saving life. I smiled too—and slept. I would remember and use her as an example years later, speaking at a nursing convocation: "Oh, the little more and how much it is. And the little less and what worlds away." She was the little more. I had seen medicine at its best.

This was not a time of taking x-rays during pregnancy, so while doing the surgery, my doctor explored my gallbladder—no stones, only scar tissue—no reason to chance more complications by removing it. In my short body with so little room between ribs and hips, I must have carried my babies in a position where they pummeled my poor gallbladder with every kick. I would not have to worry about that again. But then I hemorrhaged. Blood under my diaphragm. Outrageous pain. What but Demerol every four hours? Mel came with hugs and cards from the girls, had to rush back to take on homework and bedtime. I was hardly conscious of his coming or going.

By night, I was a zombie, full of fear and hallucinations. The TV screen high on the wall across from me had seemed at first a brand-new luxury. Now its grey face became an eye, gathered liquid and began to drip in sticky globules, over and over. I knew what I was seeing was not real, but I kept seeing it. Shivering, I thought I would never go home to see my husband or girls again. I would be mad, institutionalized. I knew it was the Demerol. I called my brother, "Homer, I can't have another shot. Help. Please. Bring Mother, I need her." When some poor intern came in with his needle I said, "No. Never again!"

Mother did come. My brother made arrangements and sides were put up on my bed. This time no joyful birthing and graduation from pain. Not even my baby to hold. Now a withdrawal still anchored in pain. No relief. Only Mother beside me as she had been when I was a little girl needing comfort. We didn't talk. I writhed and clung to the slatted iron sides of my bed and closed my eyes against the horror of the TV. I remember nothing of the next five days, except that at some point I was helped to the window to look down six stories to wave at Mel and my girls waving up from the curb.

When I finally went home, I held my baby and tried to remember how she had felt in my arms those two days before the surgery, how she had seemed more precious than breathing or being out of pain. Now, grey days of returning to myself. I was in withdrawal. For two months, I struggled with the most ordinary keeping of a house, let alone anything beyond. Then, on Mother's Day, our very knowing bishop asked me to give a talk in sacrament meeting. What had been so easy through all the years set me aquiver with anxiety. As I spoke from the pulpit, sweat soaked my blouse and my hands shook. I gave a talk about gratitude—for my family, my friends, doctors, nurses, and my Heavenly Father. I had been to Hades and come back. Mothering could be again my favorite thing.

I was one of the very lucky ones who had no gene for addiction. My need for Demerol had been situational, and after months of recovery—not a lifetime as many are condemned to—the need went away as the pain went away. But I will always have a giant understanding of that world of need, of being propelled by nothing except the screaming desire for another shot. I can rationalize that I only did what the doctors said I should, but deep in my heart lay the shudder of blame for not having had more fortitude, more faith, more anything that might have saved my baby from going through the same thing I did. After my accident three decades later, when I was still feeling remorseful, out of the night came a poem explaining that she had been in on it all with me, that just as I had wanted so much for her to be born, she had been my partner in wanting to be alive. The revelation was like ambrosia to my soul. It ended:

> *This I now know:*
> *you were not uncharged, unasking, unbegging*
> *to be, sent to be.*
> *And, like me, bent on not dislodging,*
> *crying to the wispy calendar*
> *to our saving grace*
> *Not yet! Not yet! Anything but gone*
> *this perfect chance by imperfect means*
> *to say I am! I am!*

Her birth was more than forty years ago, and she is now a wife and the mother of two particularly well-enabled boys and that piquant little Emma born on my birthday. Now a social worker and a poet, my daughter, from her home with her husband and children in El Paso, wrote of remembering her innate belonging:

REFUGE

This time of year the Monarch is in Mexico.
Here when sunsets pull back the earth's warmth
and grey shadows make trees too bare for refuge
they rise, alone, like the meander of a child's balloon,
and stream with rays into another sky.

Until the butterflies gather in Eucalyptus trees
they think they are alone in their urge.
There they cluster contented in warm winds
where on the horizon a plump sun sits
that matches the blaze of orange in their wings.

There is in me the same pull that spurs the wild.
Like the current beneath the iced-over river
there is an unsettling in these walks that used to bring peace.
If the butterfly cannot temper instinct to have to leave
how can I forget the place of my matching color?

In my steps I do not see the earth below,
but am poised for flight with all that moves:
the trains, the rivers, the last Monarch to leave.
My eyes follow as far as my stretch of sky
because in their travel they might pass home.

—Megan Thayne Heath

I love what my body has been up for—to ski mountains or lakes,
to ride a horse, to play tennis in tournaments or with my family, to
be in on kundalini, to plant a garden, to frolic with friends, to read
late or stay up all night to refinish furniture or write a story. What
my body can do translates into how I would live my life or encourage
my children to.

Ski here,
    my child,
not on gentle
slopes where
the snow is
packed and
the trail
    is wide.
        Instead,
        cut through
            the trees where
            no one's tried the
            powder. Push toward
            the hill and rotate as
            you rise. No! the
            snow-plow holds
            you back.
    It's slow
    and makes
you frightened
of your turn.
Think parallel.
Stay all in one,
then learn to ski
    the fall line, always
    down. Switchback
        skiers in their
            caution
            never know
                how dropping
                with the mountain
                keeps the balance
                right and rhythm
                smooth. Don't
            watch your
                tips
        at all!
    Look past
    them at the
deep white snow,
virgin as light,
    and yours.
        Just bend,
        release.
            You,
                gravity,
                and white
                will make your peace.

— Emma Lou Thayne

As in the disappearance of a bruise, or recovery from surgery or even addiction, healing can happen in some invisible region, from the inside out. It also happens with help from the outside in—through reciprocity—as with the gentle insight of that nurse at my bedside the night before an operation to end my childbearing. As with the story of Jesus and the woman with the flow of blood. Christ tells her to go her way in peace, that her faith has made her whole; his strength, her faith—mystic reciprocity.

Faith can heal; attitude can speed the process. Recent studies show that optimism, wishing, and hope—based on knowing—can play a major role in getting well, together with help from healers in complementary medicine.

One recent November, I scared my family with three days of dizziness, double vision, spasms, and collapsing. After every test the hospital could offer, no one could understand the cause. My doctor said I could go home for Thanksgiving (all of our families were in town) when I could walk by myself to the bathroom. A physical therapist tried to help—no use. The final test was an MRA, which examines vessels, different from an MRI, which scans bones and organs. No results till the next morning, the day I wanted so urgently to leave the hospital. On the advice of a friend, I called on another friend who does craniosacral therapy.

At 8:00 p.m., she came, applied her magic hands to my head and neck and said that the vessels at the back of my brain were narrowed, that I had been so tired the week before—true, nights of 2:00 to 3:00 a.m. bedtimes—that the heart could not pump blood into my cortex. She felt for the problem, wearing a rubber glove and pressing on my palate and teeth. My vision cleared. My head, that I had described as a pumpkin with its lid off and contents removed, began to fill. In half an hour, I was sitting without impairment, and then walking—to the bathroom!

In the morning, my doctor and her resident appeared at my door to say that I had had a small stroke, a TIA—transient ischemic attack. The MRA had revealed two troubled vessels behind the carotid and that an angiogram was in order, together with a new medication that would expand the vessels but not thin my blood. I said, "Wait there," sat up, and walked to them. I wish I could have had a picture of their faces as I told them what had happened. Wonder. Delight. Then each hugged me, my skilled internist of many years saying, "Who can argue with success?" She turned to her husky resident who had been in every morning saying he'd been thinking about me all night and trying to figure out what could be the matter. "This is a woman who will not countenance any disability," she said. "She'd take the alternative any day." I told her how glad I was that she understood this. Then I asked my reserved Polish doctor, Dr. Hecht, "What now?" Her answer, beaming, "Get the hell out of here." We laughed. And on my prescription in capital letters, she wrote, "REST!"

After all those adventurous years of twenty-six surgeries; systemic calamities; reactions to atmosphere and antibiotics; five babies; head, shoulders, knees, and middle needing help—a few summers ago, I found myself with everything working and nothing hurting. Every day, living at our cabin in the mountains, I was taking on hills and stairs like a kid. I was sleeping soundly and waking to morning with birdsongs in my head. By day and by night, I was saying, "Thank you, thank you." By midsummer my thank-yous were going upward, vertically, to the divine as they always had, but now I wanted to say them horizontally to the human experts who had helped make me well. So, what better than a party for healers?

The invitation:

To celebrate being well
and because you have helped me be,
please come to dinner at our Mt. Air Cabin.
With fond appreciation,
Emma Lou

The list grew and grew. Every little while, Mel and I would remember someone, some other cure that had been helpful through the years. But forty healers? Plus their partners? There was the grassy flat by the bonfire pit and places for twenty at the picnic tables. Inside, another twenty might sit. Surely, though, not everyone could come. Some would be out of town or have other engagements.

But we kept planning for a crowd, most of whom would not know each other—surgeons, a Chinese herbalist, massage therapist, heart specialist, acupuncturist, nurse with back rubs, physical therapist, ophthalmologist, cranial-reconstruction surgeon, dentists, internists, and those who had given spiritual blessings. Some on the list had died; others had moved away. Still, I had to keep upping the number for the caterer, a luxury seldom indulged, but that would free me to be able to visit with the crowd I'd grown so fond of.

Mel came to like the idea, helped in mopping, raking, cutting wayward branches near the railing on the steep driveway. Here was an excuse to do all the undone jobs waiting for attention since our yearly cabin opening on Memorial Day. Daughters and friends cleared shelves and repaired rugs and quilts. One friend picked wildflowers from high in the canyon, out of sight; another arranged them in quaint and antiquated containers from one hundred years of canyon living. Grandsons oiled the ramp and deck, cleared the stream, and trimmed trees hanging over the flat; the little ones sanded and oiled railings, spilled, and laughed. Another friend secretly smoothed the runs and puddles in the oiling. A friend and I blacked old iron stoves and polished their nickeling. Another helped hang a flag. Other grandsons offered to shuttle guests the two miles from the gate to the cabin. My grandmother's point de Venice tablecloths came out for the serving tables. Borrowed tables and colorful cloths were set up to accommodate the more who kept saying yes to the invitation.

The menu had to be old-fashioned and "canyon-y": cheeses, homemade bread sticks, crackers, strawberries, and lime slush while everyone arrived. Then a buffet of baked country chicken with mashed potatoes and green pea gravy, homemade rolls and butter, spinach-mandarin-walnut salad, corn on the cob, and a medley of buttered broccoli, carrots, and cauliflower. And for dessert, to honor my pioneer ancestors from England (and their cut-glass punch bowl that would hold it)—mixed berry trifle.

Fifty-eight guests came, some with flowers and candy. They all moseyed about in the perfect seventy-five-degree air in the forest, listening to the stream, being taken in by the great green arena of the canyon, and finding each other most congenial company. Healers they all were, in complementary professions—the oldest, my pathfinder woman surgeon, eighty-nine; the youngest, a professional with the movement of energy, a first-time father of two days. Because his wife couldn't come, he brought his opera-star mother, who chatted with an ear-nose-and-throat man one minute and a gastrointestinal specialist the next. Mel and the family went from bonfire to screened porch, nibbling on cheese and giving tours of the bedrooms, study, and views of the sun pulling itself off the mountain across the canyon to the east.

When dinner was over, guests were all brought to sit on the screened porch within hearing of what I so wanted to say. One of our artist daughters had drawn on butcher paper with a black marker an outline of me wearing shorts and a T-shirt and had hung it in clear view. Down the sides were the names of the healers with arrows and dotted lines identifying just where they had worked their magic. Seven decades of healing, from shoulder injuries in skiing accidents to gallbladder surgery; from back surgery to tubal ligation and later, hysterectomy; from Russian giardia to pneumonia; from death experience in that freak freeway accident to mastoid surgery and a new eardrum; from an arm caught in a water-ski rope to six root canals for teeth jarred in the accident; from a TIA to blessings for spiritual reconstituting and herbal miracles for physical energizing.

In recent years, I had been a speaker at many funerals, as my husband and I and our contemporaries were fast becoming the older generation. Looking that July night at that gathering, I welcomed the chance while they and I were still here to say—before it was too late—how fond I was of them, how much respect I had. As I went down the names and told what each had done, mentioning some divine intervention, I had them stand. Some had clever remarks; all grinned. Most were much like the schoolkids whose poems I'd read as visiting poet in elementary schools—shy, blushing, happy, I think, to be recognized for the good that they do so much of the time without note, let alone praise. To each, I gave a verse intended not for those in the business of words but for these in the business of wellness:

THE HEALER

More than a head informed, inclined
to implement training, focus a mind.

More than hands full of intricate skill
in the workings of pulses, tissues, and will.

More than an intimate knowing superb
of a test or treatment, a pill, or an herb.

Far more than a scalpel, a temperature,
exams or prescriptions, or slick sinecure.

Plugged into a circuit not out there in sight,
a healer connects with an inner light

where spirit meets spirit, and heart can tell
like mine today of a self made well.

By day, night or decade, by a lifetime of years,
please hear from my canyon—Thank you, my dears.

One week later, I woke with realizing I had forgotten to thank the part of me that cooperates in the surviving:

LOVE SONG TO MY BODY AT THE END OF SUMMER

It is clear now, body. Every day can be late August,
never quite cold.

But one must learn early what you are for.

Good old leather tiger, half domesticated
by paws in pans and shoulders hung too often with beaded fur,
you may think I forget. But you do not let me.
By now I know better. I come back.

Still, you never take me not surprised, faithful one,
by how to arrive, and the pleasure of sweat,
and how to shiver away the bee.
You move to the song behind the dance.
Even after a standard, plain white, unstriped day,
you ripple in our sleep and wait, mostly unperplexed.

And when, no matter how faint, the music breathes
behind the catcalls of too much to do, you muster
almost without my inclining, potent as needing to dance,
to pace off the house, the garden of weeds, the clogged creek,
and the midnight clutch of vagrancies. You pad from
some spring, and wild, except for my importuning, go. To do it all.

When we lie down, it will be like the squirrel there,
unflagging in the last swift moving in the leaves,
August stashed in crisp piles above the dust.

I may find no way at all without your sleek taking.

Under the wrinkles that tell you no, I can hear you now
saying, "I still love you," and to time, "Leave her alone."

A longtime and pleased-to-be matriarch, thanks to my healers, I still feel loved and as if I have all the time in the world. But just in case I might not, in September, after the healers' party, there was something I needed to do. A recognition to be made of the part the canyon must play in my being, both *here* and *there*.

My canyon, where all parts of my life fuse into a mystical connection—I needed to bring something of that to where I will be buried.

It was hardly something to explain in a phone call to my cousin who happens to own a cemetery of all-flat headstones. Thirty thousand have been buried there since 1936, including my mother and father and relatives of four generations, many near the plots my brothers and husband bought decades ago, laughing enough about stacked burials and "first in, last out," that the somber seller of such properties could hardly hold the pen out fast enough for them to sign.

Could my request have seemed any more ridiculous? "Peter, could we bring down a slab of Castle Crags to make a bench for our plot, Mel's and mine?" This, when my long-secreted wish was tossed on the altar of the traditional, the wish my family could not countenance—that my ashes be scattered over the gully and wooded hillside above the cabin, where the pure stream of our water supply makes its way through moss and brief tangy meadows, curling around rocky falls to the foot of enormous, imposing, magnificent granite-like Castle Crags. That giant outcropping has overlooked our bonfire pit, our tree huts in the pines, our Tarzan swing off the mountain, our intimate acquaintance with squirrels, birds, butterflies, and snakes. So, what more reasonable? If I could not go to the canyon, why not bring the canyon to me?

And so they came, that day in early September: Peter, his landscaper, and his stonemason to see what this crazy lady had in mind. I gave them cranberry juice on the screened porch as we scanned the arena of our canyon. Then we hiked that warm day to the foot of Castle Crags, me clutching the back of Peter's belt to manage my unsteady climb. There it was, the slab broken away just below the steep final path to the enormous outcropping above us. Peter and I reminisced about climbing there as children, running on its uneven top, sitting there to throw rocks at pinecones in the trees below, taking in the view of the whole canyon.

On the pine-needle path where the sloughed-off rock lay in the shade of a thick forest, the landscaper began to plan how to winch the two-ton rock off the mountain and into a truck to take to the cemetery, there to become part of its own garden. The stonemason figured out the mounting so as not to polish or shave an edge or surface for the rock to become the bench I had so intimately imagined. Later, a marker was placed with names and dates and part of a poem from a book I'd written a quarter of my lifetime before:

> *This is my place.*
> *Finally I have turned away*
> *and walked into the morning.*
> *It is as I knew it would be:*
> *I do or I don't do.*
> *At last that is not the thing.*
> *What is this: I am here.*
> *And whatever is calling in the crags knows.*

In less than a week, they had the stone. How, I still don't know. But it lay through the winter near the toolsheds in the cemetery with its wide expanses of lawn and only trees interrupting the view to the Wasatch Range and sky. I saw the slab there on walks, and my cousin told me it would be in place by spring. Mel liked the idea and laughed, saying he had never seen me happier than when we talked about it.

On Memorial Day, as Mel and I took flowers to graves of our dear ones and asked directions to a grave we couldn't locate, my cousin grinned, saying, "Have you seen it?" We hadn't. But we followed his directions and there it was. Under its newly planted multileaf maple, in its own cutout bed of mountain privet and rose of Sharon, it stood in an irregular, elegant shape exactly that of the rock. On a firm base, it was still part of Castle Crags, rugged, untampered with, inviting anyone to sit and look up, not down. We did, smiling at each other as we watched the clouds playing over the mountains and, I swear, smiling back.

As part of our spree on his fourth birthday, our first great-grandchild and I had a picnic on the rock. Between hot dogs and root beer, we sat and told stories, and he jumped as far as he could to reach the grass beyond the planting, laughing, "See Gramma Grey, I made it!" A perfect time to explain, too, why a crowd gathered far across the green to honor someone else; time to make the idea of my death not something to be afraid of; time for the healing from fear that I would offer anyone at any age.

The body and the spirit, the sometimes separation, the ultimate reunion—the final healing. And the bequeathing, like the matriarchs in my life, to supply rich nourishment for new generations to grow by:

NURSE LOG

In the rain forest where the spiked hand
of lightning or stiff old age rattles a day
or night until stout trees no longer stand,
the Sitka spruce lies down to rich decay
and takes on another life. It will replace
itself five fold by offering a sapling fir
or spruce a straddling of its furrows twice
as sure as earth. It spreads the musky word
and cultivates its bed. Seed tells root. More
youngsters swing their leggy crotches and get
astride. These children, so enriched, can soar
on limbs and air their predecessors fed.
Sweet comfort for bequeather of the breath!
Far from sacrifice this giving life in death.

Sometimes writing a silly poem just for fun can be as healing as any treatment. One morning, I lay in bed thinking of all the parts I'd lost to surgery. I smiled in bringing them back:

DITTY TO MY MISSING PARTS

Where are you waiting, my missing contraptions?
Parts so long in on my acts and reactions?
We'll be reunited in that other life
but meantime I'm lacking what's gone with the knife.

First tonsils at four, appendix at twenty,
since, gall bladder, uterus, moles more than plenty.
An eardrum, a breast, and wisdom teeth, so
are they consorting today with my nipped second toe?

Where are my actual left hip and right knee?
With substitute fixtures, is what's left really me?
Does my lost stuff know physiology?
And the source of its real genealogy?

Do items out there know they're all related?
Does time of departure say how situated?
With so much I was born with now distant collection
is restitution included in resurrection?

So I've been taught and I know that it's true
but will they all fit and say, "Boy we missed you!"

CHAPTER 9

THE INEFFABLE
SHARED

We can make our minds so like still water that beings gather about us that they may see, it may be, their own images, and so live for a moment with a clearer, perhaps even with a fiercer life because of our quiet.

—W. B. Yeats

On one of my visits in Sun Valley, I was trying to sort out the whys of this book, still wanting to understand what had happened to me after the accident. Suddenly, the keyboard on my computer blew. The whole machine had run amok. It was too much static electricity from the deep carpet under the dining room table—not exactly chosen as proper grounding for a machine. I took my ailing keyboard two miles away to Ketchum. Hoping to have it fixed in half a day and ready to get back to work, I left the computer repair shop and walked three blocks to Chapter One Bookstore. Why not something interesting for my waiting—a book, a magazine?

Instead, something drew me to the back of the shop: Akasha Organics juice bar. Why not some juice for lunch? Behind the counter smiled a slim, tanned guru of vegetable and fruit concoctions. He might have been a reincarnation of a '60s hippie, except that he was anything but. I knew immediately that he was much more than a wanderer. His smile spread like light from a torch, part of an energy as contagious as it was disarming. I had learned many times about the possibilities in chance meetings, and I instantly trusted this one to be a great adventure. I was not to be disappointed. His name was Ananda.

Not of my world, I think. Not this man in compact, billowy motion behind the wooden stools and bar. He is a presence, with brown-grey ponytail, tiny stud earrings, wide purple pants, an ochre turtleneck, long sleeved to ringless hands that are feeding greens, beets, carrots, celery, and ginger into the gulping, noisy, metal juicer.

"Everything becomes present tense," I think. He pushes his offerings into the upturned maw of the machine. He drops and presses unrecognizable stems and leaves, then quarters unpeeled apples, tomatoes, and parsley with offhand attention, his brown gaze on me. Without knowing, I know that what pours into his glass blender is not reduced but metamorphosed. He pours it into a towering paper cup. He smiles—"A salad in a glass." I smile and drink salad. We are friends with no distance between us.

Above the contours of shelves, utensils, and refrigerated innards of organic juice, heroic pink male and female figures with wings in a white-and-blue universe are painted. They blend with my Mormon Moroni and Mary at Christ's tomb. I believe Ananda's unspoken question to Mary Magdalene would not be "Why weepest thou?" but "How shinest thou?" He invites rendezvous with some bright spirit I am only starting to claim.

I tell him what I am writing and something about my death experience. He says I must visit a natural temple two hours from any-where, atop the sage desert of Shoshone, Idaho. Indians worshiped there in seven temples ten thousand years ago. We would visit only one—it would take a week to visit all seven. I would try to find a way to go.

"Ananda's the best skater anywhere around—and a holy man,"

says my crisp, white-haired friend of the valley. "He was a downhill racer, lightning on the ski hill once—skates from here eighty miles to Mountain Home." When I learn about Ananda's Rollerblading, I ask him where he practices and go to watch him in the Mormon Church parking lot at noon. His head in a turbanlike swatch of red and orange, his body slim as a muscular woman, he is dancing alone, smiling. He is a picture of grace and peace amid the wild antics of a dozen teenagers trying tricks on skateboards and shouting over the roar of wheels on asphalt. He skates by me close enough to say, "Maybe if I skate here enough, in my next life I'll be Mormon."

"I already am," I say.

"I know," Ananda says. But how? I'd never told him. No matter.

Yes, he'd raced; a downhill skier, he'd fallen, broken his leg, and learned from a surgeon in Denver about Hinduism. Since he was nine, he had been reading the likes of Indian poet Tagore and found healing. I had university students who would be baffled by Tagore. For a quarter of a century, Ananda had crossed the map as a monk. Then another kind of peace called to him and he was back in the earthy West to be a gardener and then operator of the juice bar. Still celibate, richly alive, he teaches yoga and Hindu philosophy to locals, offering his spiritual acquisitions like juices made by hand to celebrate a wellness green as moss.

"When did you learn to skate?"

"Not till I was fifty."

"You're how old now?" One leg aloft behind him, he skates backward to the tree I sit against.

"Oh, fifty-two or there about."

"Twenty years exactly from where I'll be October 22nd."

"Great. The age every Hindu aspires to be."

"Seventy-two?"

"Yes. From birth to twenty-four—infancy, student. From twenty-four to forty-eight—householder, life work, family. Forty-eight to seventy-two—beginning to know, retirement. Seventy-two—*Sannyasa ashrama*—contemplative, to the Hindu, wisdom, spirit, time."

I like the idea a lot.

Two weeks and I would be loading up to drive home, but not without seeing the Lava Dome. Needing to wait until he closes the juice bar, Ananda arranges the trip for after sundown—for the two of us and two young men and a woman who want to visit the hollow temple. After a two-hour drive in the Suburban belonging to one of the men, we strangers climb for another hour in the twilight to the temple. Sagebrush and wildflowers snap beneath the boots Ananda had told us to wear—with pants tucked in to keep mosquitoes out. Dizzy since my accident, over the bumpy hillside I cling to the back of his red parka to maintain my footing and ask, "How did you know this was here?"

"Some psychic was driving up Highway 84 not thinking about it at all and felt vibrations that drew him to the spot."

Would anything less have fit? The dome rises like a mini Mormon tabernacle. We heave ourselves up the last incline. "Think of someone you especially want to be influenced by your meditations" is Ananda's only instruction.

We scramble inside, five strangers scattered by circumstance and preference, sitting together there in the silence of after sundown. I back myself against a wall and try not to let my fused back scream into my quiet. I have no idea where the others are, so deep is the dark. Crooked oval openings to the east and west close time into ebony too intense to see except for black sky giving way to stars. The horizon on the west tells what earth says to sky, what sky says back in the hushing of birds, the nip of sage still in our noses.

The hard impermanence of the dirt floor sets memories afloat in my palms and soles. "Its own kundalini," I think. An owl, close, wails on the night like the universe alive. The imponderable good luck of an owl. The voice of no wind, of minutes untimed as breath, holds me like the roots of my hair growing unperceived, my history in motion in every capillary. The gush of tension running out, the quieting of an hour of nonlanguage becomes all the words I have struggled to tell. The dance of being electric with plans or purpose is released in a steady heartbeat, a pulse in my throat. The hour is as separate as sleeping, as fond as caress, as unneedy as childness, as settled as stars on the move in the night. Every thought disappears except for sending my warmest prayers for my daughter in her time of anguish.

Without a word, Ananda stands, more felt than visible. We all follow him from the Lava Dome. Again I clutch the slick red back of his parka as he guides my uncertain feet through the hillocks of sage, erupting anthills, and the tang of wildflowers. Flashlights of the three others arrow far ahead, young, quicker with departures. The vast space blacks out behind them.

"Thank you for time in the temple of those ancients," I say.

"It was right," he says, "that you should come here. I knew you would not be afraid."

His boots take on the uneven slope, not fast, not slow, unmeasured as the pulse of his Rollerblades. From Zen, Ananda explains, spiritual understanding is *samadhi—the way*. It is peace of mind. There is no searching after it. Vast and boundless, samadhi is an experience, not a conceptual understanding. An experience. I know my daughter far away will be healed of her trouble. And I—I know my travel will be winged, organic, right. The gift of silence tingles in my palms and fingers as I hold and feel for footings in the dark.

Back in my retreat, alone, my book was becoming pages from the night and now from beyond the Shoshone Ice Caves. The pages drew my hand along their lines like Ananda's sure descent from the dome where we five sat with the desert. It was Ananda who would introduce me as "one who was hit by a spear from the gods." We would be in touch ever after.

St. Nicholas Cathedral, Galway, Ireland—a tourist must-see and an unlikely setting for my coming full circle back to my experience with death. Here I would have a beyond-earthly experience with life— an experience that would teach me the shareability of the mystic, the reason for this book.

On our last full day in Ireland, two of us six writers invited for twelve days to a thatched cottage on Galway Bay sat that late afternoon in the hardwood-backed pew of a vast hall. White sculptures of the Stations of the Cross banked the upward curve of the walls. As with Paul Fini's Stations, behind each I saw pure emotion splashed like the brilliant stained-glass windows on the west caught by the sun. Rainbows, almost as defined as the huge one over our cottage in Connemara that had started our day, now danced on the great stone pillars under the far ceiling of matching wood. The station of Christ speaking to the women hung over us to the right. At the same time, in astonishing synchronicity, and at what seemed like miles ahead of us, plain white light streamed through other windows to the crucifix where an artist's Christ hung and two unidentifiable figures knelt.

"We can't leave until the light leaves," I said to my friend. "It's too unbelievable."

We had made our way, at my friend's suggestion, across the cathedral parking lot where our rental car waited. We'd come from a laughter-filled visit to the legendary Kenny's Book Shop and Art Gallery to buy ancient maps of where her progenitors had lived in Northern Ireland, and for me, the poems of Eavan Boland and Mary O'Malley, new Irish inspirations.

"This can't be a walk-through," we'd decided upon approaching the cathedral, even though we had a schedule to keep. Families of Irish friends would be coming to the cottage for our American friends' barbecued spareribs, coleslaw, and blackberry pie. From fluffy Irish potatoes that wouldn't cube, I'd promised mashed-potato salad, all of us smiling at what an evening of Irish merriment portended.

On our way inside, we had passed a scattering of worshipers in a small chapel, holding a celebration of the Eucharist. Beyond that, no more than ten or twelve occupied the cathedral. A hush echoed like prayer. "It's not so much the place or the mode of worship," I whispered, awed by the beauty of the centuries-old church. "It's the impulse to revere something holy." This was not my first reverie in a cathedral, but it was to be like no other.

Ireland was different. My friend and I, we two Mormon women a generation apart—she, in her forties, I, in my seventies—had, as we crossed the bridge over the river to the cathedral, talked of our believing, where we stood, where our lives had taken us, and about how we had come as writers invited to Ireland. Alike and different, the talk still in our heads, we settled into our private accesses to what shone there. Through our days at the cottage, we six had read to each other from our writings, I, from "Meditations on the Heavens." I had told about relaxing my temples just before sleep to invite what the night might offer, what my muse, my Holy Ghost never failed to bring as comfort and inspiration as I slept. Despite warm efforts of mine to teach it, and theirs to do it, no one had figured out how. Now, sitting in the cathedral, I relaxed my temples and asked my companion of the afternoon if she could do the same.

Looking straight ahead, she relaxed into a posture of meditation. Gradually, almost transfixed, she whispered, "Look, I'm doing it!"

"Now think of your palms. Do they feel any different?"

She sat, palms up, with her hands in front of her. "Yes. There is a warmth."

Kundalini had already warmed the soles of my feet and my palms when suddenly, from nowhere, the music came, a woman's, then women's, voices singing "Danny Boy" in Gaelic.

"That's my song," I murmured. Could it be true? That song here? Now? "I learned it for my father when I was ten; it's the only thing I still can play on the piano. It was at my father's funeral, and my mother's. It will be at mine." Every word I knew, every phrase settled in my remembering like the gentleness of my parents' beloved hands. I bowed my head as tears streamed down my face and onto my shirt, only the fervent yes of knowing they were there, in the engulfing light of the cathedral. To the third and last verse:

But if ye come
And all the flowers are dying
If I am dead, as dead I well may be,

Ye'll come and find
The place where I am lying
And bend and say an Ave there for me.

And I shall hear
Though soft you tread above me
And all my grave
Will warmer, sweeter be,
For you will bend and whisper that you love me
And I shall sleep in peace until you come to me.

I was filled with the light. I had experienced kundalini often, but this was something far beyond the usual. The ecstasy of my death experience returned. My Catholic friend in Tulsa told me later that we had heard the "music of the spheres," a phenomenon known in her world but seldom experienced. She said, too, that for that time I "rested in the Spirit," again something of a rarity.

My friend in the cathedral later said she had looked at her watch to see the time, wondering about vespers. Or a choir? A secular song in a cathedral? It was just after seven, no ritual moment, no sight of anyone, no source visible for music. Later, she described "the sun awash on the crucifix and Christ, the room expands to take in spirit, connection, lineage, and glory." For seventeen minutes, she watched my trance as I filled with the same light that filled the hall, breathing deeply and then hardly at all, coasting as I do in sleep to where light originates, lofted now by the essence of all the dears who came near—childness alive in every pore.

When the music stopped, disappeared, I could not move. Not another note, but still no clue as to its source. When I finally could open my eyes, the cathedral was empty. Only my friend and I remained. Had anyone else heard the music? As with the vision in the painting in the nave of my childhood church—the vision not painted there—I did not want to ask or know. Did the artist put it in, the vision, or did I? We left the cathedral slowly. I thought of

Luke 11:36: "If thy whole body therefore be full of light, having no part dark, the whole shall be full of light, as when the bright shining of a candle doth give thee light."

Back at the cottage, we were not ready for the party, now well underway. I went to my room to watch for the moon while my friend took to clearing the kitchen. When another friend came for me, I went to the children's table to visit, a stepping-stone into the merriment of the adults gathered by a peat fire. The men sang of Galway Bay and Irish eyes, and we laughed through "I've Been Working on the Railroad." Songs for hours, and a daughter of the man in charge of horses did river dancing on our red, quarry-tile floor—never a party of more gaiety—Irish gaiety.

After they left, we six writers took to the verandah to watch the purple clouds uncover the half moon. Still entranced, three wandered off to bed. But I couldn't let go of the day. One friend stoked the peat fire, one sat beside me for a while, and I stayed wrapped in an Irish shawl, eventually alone until 4:00 a.m.—burning eyes unwilling to close, some spirit alive in me as I had forgotten it could be.

———

When I reached home, Rachel told me in a reading that my chakras looked as if "God had turned up the lights, and you are set aside to touch hearts and speak to souls. Always that luminosity was at the core. Now it's out. It has come out at different times but receded."

My trip to Ireland was what Rachel called "soul-retrieval work." From some ancient piece of Celtic lineage, I had absorbed truth speaking in a rhythm, a poetry. I was translating the vibration, she said, revitalized by lots of bright yellow-green, a wash of colors, all of it harmonizing.

Just thinking about it now, writing about it all this time later, I am still occupied by the holiness. I radiate and quiver, my temples relax without instruction to the coming together of the earthly and the metaphysical, the groundwork laid through all my more than seventy years, Ireland the catalyst.

Had it begun as a child with my Sunday morning imbibing of Joseph Smith's vision? At twenty-two, I had received my traditional once-in-a-lifetime blessing by a Mormon patriarch. At the time, it was disappointing to me, primarily because it said nothing about my becoming "a mother in Zion" as all of my friends' blessings had. I had dismissed the blessing for years as too general to matter as my life filled with not only being a wife and mother but with a world of people and places within the church and without that enriched my every capacity. On returning from Ireland, for some reason I read the blessing again. One paragraph, more than fifty years old, came alive:

> to seek Him in season and out of season and not forget to petition Him in secret and tell Him of your difficulties and your impressions and your desires to let your light shine among your relatives and your associates. Your obligation is to love Him above all other things, with great whole heart, with all your mind and strength, and if you will put Him first in your love, His blessings shall be with you and surround you, and you shall have great happiness.

Over the decades since, what a continuum of offerings from dissimilar sources: generations of believers and matriarchs, from grandmas to Mother; Lowell Bennion and his Mormon rootings in the vertical and the horizontal, the divine and the human; Paul Fini and his Catholic Stations of the Cross; Rachel's finding Eastern knowing and luminescence in my auras; my writing a hymn from an extremity of need, asking, "Where can I turn for peace?" and learning as I wrote, "He answers privately, reaches my reaching."

"The story is a map," Rachel told me—my journey a map for others. "Recollecting in tranquility" my time in Ireland, I know now that it is possible to share the gift of the mystic with another of like intent, availability, openness to light. My purpose is to bring others to this assurance. It need not take a crowbar through a windshield. The awakening can be in places made holy by taking note in the pores.

| CHAPTER 10 |

^{ON} PAYING ATTENTION

You come back one nanosecond or something at a time after you leave, so to any neutral observer you never left at all.

—Carl Sagan

Since my accident, the nanoseconds, the smallest measure of time of my being back, mount up to years as the mystical connections multiply like stars in the heavens. Days go by so fast I can't live them. Only reflection saves their gifts to my life. I hope this book makes clear that they are there for anyone, the small miracles. But only through paying attention can we respect and retain what is there to awaken us, to guide us to a state of realization. "Lucky lady, Lulie," my journal says over and over. The gifts. The observable offerings from the divine and the human—Lowell's vertical and horizontal turns—continue if I simply take time to notice the subtle destiny.

It would have been easy to miss him. About four feet tall—as kids would say, below the radar. His mother, a distinguished former legislator, approached me as we left a funeral for Vickie, beloved fifty-eight-year-old leader of NAMI, the association for attention to the mentally ill. She had been killed when her car rolled on unexpected ice in a canyon on her way to give a talk about how to help. A pillar of caring, who could take her place? Heart sad, I was hurrying from conversations to my car and an appointment with a doctor. Vickie's favorite hymn, sung at the funeral, resonated in my leaving: "Each life that touches ours for good / Reflects thine own great mercy, Lord."

"Hello." I didn't recall the name of the woman who spoke to me, as happens often now. "You were there when we got the bill for mental health insurance out of committee."

I remembered. "Oh yes. Thank you for sponsoring it. It made Vickie very happy to have that passed."

"This is my son." She looked down toward the boy in a white shirt and dark tie, his sleeves buttoned.

"Hello," I said, smiling but not knowing what to expect from an obviously Down's syndrome child. "What's your name?"

He looked away from me, searched the sky, and began to say . . .

"Richard," his mother supplied.

"Mom, don't do that! I know!" His agitation boiled in his slanted blue eyes.

"Richard!" I exclaimed, catching his glance. "That's the name of my brother! What a great name! How old are you?"

Searching the sky again and then looking at me, he said, "Twenty-two. Soon twenty-three."

"Terrific," I said, surprised at how old he was. "And when is your birthday?"

By now we were connecting. Looking right at me, he started, "Ock . . . Ock . . ."

"October?" I grinned. "That's my birthday month too. We're pals!" I put my hand out and he shook it, his square hand and stubby fingers filling mine, smiling hard around slightly crooked teeth.

I wanted a hug.

"What day in October?"

Now he was searching the sky again, his mouth pursed, his eyes squinting, his hands at the sides of his cheeks.

"October twenty-second," his mother supplied again. Before he could care, I exclaimed, "Not really?! That's my birthday too! Give me five!" He was beaming as he slapped my outstretched hand. "And my final grandbaby was born on that same day and named for me— Emma." He kept smiling right at me. "When she learned to talk, she called our birthday 'twenty-tober-second.'" I grinned to him. He just kept smiling as his mother grinned too. "Now we're really friends. We'll have to say hello on our birthday. You'll be twenty-three and I'll be eighty-one. Wow!"

Others approached his mother and him. "He doesn't talk to strangers much," she said. He and I grinned at each other again. He kept grinning as I turned to get my car. His smile rode with me. Richard, thank you. Every time I need a boost, I'll think "Richard," and that smile will light my day, or night.

He made me think of Emma too. On October 22, 1997, on my seventy-third birthday, she, our final grandbaby, was born to be named Emma Grace. I was invited to be in on her coming. She arrived under a double rainbow beyond the window of the hospital birthing room, her mother, dad, and I in ecstatic tears; her two brothers, ten and eight, taking turns holding their blanketed tiny sister, grinning like Richard just now.

In only one day, she came home to a household eager to claim her. That night beside her crib, I took up my much-anticipated assignment. As with other newborn grandchildren, I got to sleep with her cradle beside me, be on call when she woke, change her and take her to her mother down the hall. We were companions at hours otherwise reserved for sleep.

So little crying in her, she wakes me with movement more than sound to what I suppose to be uncompromising readiness for her mother's milk. On the changing table, her silken, minute bottom is dry. Her eyes, quizzical and calm, seem to return my happy, sleepy gaze, then turn to find another place: Emma, two days old, meditates. For half an hour at a time, Emma Grace lies looking at the white wall. All is there beyond her. Elfin hands butterfly the air. Grasshopper legs untighten, stretch, pump a gentle paean to arrival. Eyes not yet supposed to see search out a somewhere, blinking in stillness. She will repeat this wonderment every night for the five I am there. Her quiet folds her *here* into the *there* a white wall must exude. I hum a hymn by Eliza R. Snow, written early in Mormon history, "O my Father . . . / In thy holy habitation, Did my spirit once reside? / In my first primeval childhood, / Was I nurtured near thy side?"

At the other end of life a quarter century earlier, I had written of Grandmother Emma Louise Stayner Richards's death, "Angel, angel, snowy angel, spread your wings and fly." Now, after Emma's birth, with no precedent, my grandma comes for me. Out of Sunday morning dark, my grandma at seventy-nine, the age I knew her last, beckons me. Given over to lucid dreaming, I see her occupy the fat, black leather rocker then in her sitting room, now in ours, where my uncle lifted her from bed and Mother helped her dress for her last time up before the liver cancer took her. Her long velvet dress, blue-on-blue, and amber beads I know, like her hand that reaches for mine, a twelve-year-old's. Her hand is identical to mine now at seventy-nine—tawny, veined, with fingers straight, bones obvious on the cushioned leather arms. I slide my smaller child's hand to where she covers it with hers and presses, anointing me with her smile between the hollow cheeks, her deep brown, claiming eyes still holding me these sixty-seven years since our last touch.

To church that morning, I wore my blue-on-blue dress, ten years hung away since our last daughter's wedding, with my grandma's amber beads, untouched till then in my dresser drawer. The grandma that I have become is a lighted shell, housing like the sun in trees, the limber spirit of a girl touched holy by a holy visit in the night.

Certainty claimed me. Again I knew by Eliza R. Snow's hymn, "When I leave this frail existence, / When I lay this mortal by, /

Father, Mother, may I meet you / In your royal courts on high? / . . . With your mutual approbation / Let me come and dwell with you."

We are our stories—dozens, hundreds, thousands of them—sprayed across our memories, embedded in our identity. Calling them up for others or for ourselves or for God, can enlighten, crush, amuse, trap, or free us, depending on how we pay attention. Once when I talked with a daughter about paying attention, that any life could be richer for being examined, she said:

> Mother, don't you know that 90 percent of us live 99 percent of the time simply in the experience? In all the rush, who has the time even for the inclination, let alone the chance, ever to do more? Oh, would I love to.

Later, I thought, "Hon, you're right." How many ever get a chance to reflect, to process as I had in the alone time just afforded me in my retreat? And how many might even want to? Beyond that, how many live not even in their own experience, but in the experience of others? Like children before the television—a "virtual life," consequently with the need to copy, to act out, to try to make vicarious experience personal, totally unacquainted with themselves. Yet expansion is born of curiosity and suggests endless possibilities, given even a little time. What it takes is that first step: paying attention. Attention to experience that becomes a story of our own.

A WALK INTO SEVENTY

Yesterday on my nippy October walk
I picked two dandelions beside the path.
The first was still a yellow starburst
barely poking out from under the dead grass,
hiding from what the seasons had to say.
It had fooled the wind and slanted sun so well
it had staved off turning into a puff of grey

like the second one I picked,
round, delicate, standing upright on its stem,
a constellation that might in any wind explode.

I put them on my desk where,
lying on a yellow aspen leaf,
they could stay the night.
Next morning,
the yellow dandelion was limp,
stem and all,
shriveled to no sign of what it was.

The grey was still intact, virtually unchanged by being picked,
as if it needed no nourishment except from itself, inside.
One edge has lost some wisps, thinned out.
But its basics are definable, a constellation still,
on a wrinkled but pliable stem.
It could yet go with the wind in a hundred directions,
drop the bounty of its intricate remnants,
tiny umbrellas to send into spring.

Maybe that's what being seventy implies,
what a woman poet says, "I must notice then
and write of all the small glories in my life."

And then let them scatter as they will.

We have amazing and too-seldom-paid-attention-to allies.

Our first ally is *luck*—the chance happening of good or bad events; random, haphazard events outside ourselves. That first contact with random experience can go unnoticed. With something as simple as a dandelion by the trail or my moment with Richard that afternoon after a funeral, *noticing* can offer light in my life. The earth and its offerings, like all people, are sacred, whatever race, age, color, religion, setting, or seeming capacity. Each has something to bring to the music of humanity. We need only to listen to let that music inform and inspire us, as we relish our luck and reflect on our experience.

A second ally is *synchronicity*. Beyond luck, seeming coincidences can alter our lives. Our world is evolving, and if we're awake, so are we. Some would say nothing is by accident. Big or little synchronicities touch us with timely yes! A car pulling out of the parking space in front of where you were late for an appointment. Opening to the right scripture or line from a poem for the exact moment of need. A friend on the phone just as you hoped for a call. To capitalize on any experience, we must be open to newness even as we let the past flow into the present to guide us in how to accept or reject the new. Love is the catalyst for seeing human potential or a chance to make a difference.

Our third and most unacknowledged ally is *divine grace*. Just as I learned to know it in my accident and recovery, I can be certain of its presence always. I realize that most of life happens to me alone. Though I have had hands on my head for blessing, loved ones to hold and guide me, human pillars to sustain my faith, a sea of support to let me be all I can be, my living is done only by me and my spirit. But soul, character, inner impulse, and choosing are directly influenced by divine accompaniment.

Sometimes we have all three elements of the mystic alive in a relationship—luck, synchronicity, and divine grace. All have come into play with another friend Edith. She was there, nearly thirty years younger than I was in my first time away, in that poetry symposium with Maxine Kumin in Port Townsend, Washington. The best poet in the group, she shone without effort, a darkly beautiful, brilliant, shy star who would later get an advanced degree in poetry from the prestigious Iowa Writers' Workshop. What kind of luck was mine the second day of our workshop to find on my scanty desk in my solitary, unlocked room in the barracks, a perfect sand dollar; under it, written on a paper napkin, "From Edith"? Who was Edith? Stranger to the whole experience, I knew no names in our group. The next day in class, we read our sonnet assignments; mine about my big brother and sailing, Edith's, a sensitive yet unsentimental description of a four-year-old's dimpled hand. I liked it. I liked her. Thanks to the sand dollar and her willingness to chance leaving it on my desk, we became friends. She invited me into the mystique of the San Juans, the fog before sunrise shrouding every stem or branch with gossamer mystery as the foghorns wailed. My roots ran from my Wasatch Mountains to her chilly sea.

In years to come, she would visit my canyon on a snowmobile, charming my family and friends with tales of working in hip boots canning salmon in Alaska in summer to make money to free her to live in the San Juans and write in the winter. ("Never eat canned salmon," she admonished with a smile.) She would invite me to Iowa to hear Nobel winner Czeslaw Milosz read poetry and send me strangely tender poems by prisoners in a program she taught in Connecticut. Then the synchronicity.

Out of touch except for maybe a yearly phone call, I learned that that year she was celebrating her fiftieth birthday by having one hundred friends on a pleasure boat on Lake Washington. Why didn't I come? Why not! I even had that perfect sand dollar with her note to take to be displayed among the memorabilia of her other friends from Connecticut to Montana, from Alaska to Los Angeles. This would be a festivity unlike any ward dinner I could remember in Salt Lake City. Musicians from one of her adopted families came from New York. People she wanted most for me to meet were her Native American family from Montana and the excavator, cutter of paths in her woods, and builders of her long wished–for island home, who had become her friends. The day after the party, she drove me to take the ferry to the island.

Here was the exotic beauty of the San Juans and the sea, also the verdant tranquility of my mountain home. Grass-centered trails cut through the forest and down to the rocky beach; tucked into vales and secret openings, benches and seats of hand-hewn wood invited sublime pausing. Birds sprang from bushes and trees and sang at the top of their voices. Later, as we searched the heavens, walking the dirt road in the dark, somewhere coyotes howled at the new moon and deer crashed through thickets. Edith enlarged my perceptions—like teaching me to walk in the dark.

At the cabin years ago, I learned from Grandma the excitement of turning off lights to see the sky. The eye can see farther than any light can shine. But a flashlight had been my friend forever. Edith taught me that other senses can interpret the dark even more distinctly, by trusting the feel of footing, the sound of silence, the penetrable distance between objects near and far, the scent of the familiar and the unfamiliar. Mystics talk about a third eye that can perceive auras and intentions. Edith uses multisensory sensations to walk any path on her island preserve without even the light of the moon. It was catching, her trust in what animals enjoy that we human beings have long neglected in our dependence on only sight. Paying attention. Edith at fifty would be the same knowing companion in the poetry of place that she had been in Port Townsend twenty years before.

And then the divine grace. Discouraged, disheartened at the editing of the manuscript of my mystic life by someone capable but not on the same wavelength, I had snatched this book from the jaws of the presses. "You'll lose the magic," my friend Laurel warned when I complained about not being in sync with what was happening to my manuscript, different than any editing I usually welcomed. As is often my rescue, I was pumping out my despair on our recumbent bike in the downstairs playroom and with closed eyes imploring, "Where can I turn for peace?" The phone rang. It was Edith. Before she had a chance to say why she was calling, I spilled out my anguish.

"Would you like me to edit it for you?" Edith, edit? Edith, my spiritual guru who had been first to tell me about mystic connections, who understood how to walk in the dark, who was rooted in extraordinary poetry and brought up in traditional belonging? What kind of privilege was she suggesting? Edit? For me? "I'd want to pay you," I blurted. Edith laughed. "Absolutely not!" She laughed again.

"The only thing I'd want is for you to be completely honest in your story. I think you're hiding."

She was right. I had been telling only surface stuff, true but not deep. As my daughters had said, "You make it sound too easy, Mother. And not for everyone." I would trust Edith's intuitive reading of my book. Now she was saying she wanted the book to be all it could be. I was ecstatic. All I could say in my journal and on my knees that night was "thank you."

———

We can invite divine influence at any time. Not necessarily on my knees or in a prescribed setting, I find prayer can be as natural as breathing. Maybe since my accident, it has been as if the divine is breathing with me, aware of what I'm about, no need for words, let alone intermediary. What I know is that anyone is eligible for this kind of connecting. All that is needed is letting it be. God is waiting on us, beyond our touching, like Adam in the Sistine Chapel, in our very human awareness and trust.

Anchored in that trust, I can live by my own unique truth. As can anyone, each with his or her own prayers and answers. It does not happen only to the chosen few. In living by essence, in the childness that allows us to connect to the essence of others, we can abide in the place of no fear. This is the truth of my story. It continues. We can be emissaries for that influence. That was my promise in returning from the place of knowing. It can be as simple as being appreciative.

After an operation to replace my damaged hip, I was very slow in recovering. Nearly eighty-five, I was having to face that I may not be as resilient as always. Discouraged, I lay in my bed in the rehab center wondering, "Would I ever be myself again?" Through the door came a troop of little kids from our neighborhood, six of them with their teacher from Primary. I knew them from being a greeter at church and also from tossing balls with them on the lawn in front of our house. "We brought you this," a boy about eight announced as he handed me a shoe box wrapped in white paper and decorated with crayon hearts and flowers. Children's printing in bright colors said, "You cool!", "You rock!", "Fantastic!", "Way to go!" amongst their very large signatures and "With Love."

"Wonderful!" I smiled. "What have you brought me?"

Inside the box, gifts were wrapped in hand-printed scriptures: a tiny flashlight with "And your light shall shine." And a bar of soap with "He that hath clean hands and a pure heart..." They were smiling and giving me hugs saying, "Get better! We miss you!" What a way to bring life to a very old lady! What a gracious and funny route to healing. Reciprocity—another kind of paying attention.

Our annual birthday sprees are my chance to know my grand-children, and now also my great-grandchildren, and they to know me. With their ages spread from three to thirty-six, we get to intersect with each other's lives, equal in paying attention, for two to three hours a year.

By the time we sit across from each other at a place offering their favorite shrimp, steak, Chinese, Mexican, Italian, or vegan fare, we are ready for each other's stories. We cover school, marriage, sports, friends, excitements, and discouragements. I swoon at their latest fear-factor escapades on bikes, skateboards, or snowboards, and they hear about my going over a cliff on skis. Their pets, their books, their dreams of a trip or dread of a test, their losses or wins in a game or election occupy us as my recollections make us laugh or extend our understanding of a crisis. Along the way, someone brings up talk of believing and belonging, often of gratitude for being in on love.

In our final hug, I marvel at how they grow past me. I picture them as in the kundalini of my seeing them in my drive home from Sun Valley. I have their stories tucked in with mine. In our quickening, we have become authentic to one another. We have paid attention.

At the deepest level of being, I know I am one with all that is. Despite, or maybe because of, my encounter with the place of knowing, I have learned that being in touch and paying attention needs to be a constant. That, especially when I need it most, inspiration has to come from a source beyond myself. I have to be always aware of the stillness, the inner kind of listening that I learned to hear in the months after my accident, when I could not read or be part of my usually busy outer life.

The blessing of intercedence can come in many forms. For me, the night and then stillness will make their offerings. I know I must save a lovely morning of waking slowly, for protection against days when I am jarred awake with a list mentality, not having time to know who has been to visit in the night. Even then, I must relish the wholeness of seeing without seeing, hearing without hearing, of going by feel toward something holy—of knowing it can be there for anyone willing to pay attention. For me—in growing from Highland Park Ward to Israel to Ireland; in Russia, Romania, China, or the Amazon jungle; from the birth of babies to the death of loved ones; in learning, in teaching, in skiing a hill, in building a cabin; in being held, in holding, in healing, in loving and being loved; on earth and in the heavens; in the ineffable journey of body, mind, and spirit, the wholeness is there, available, waiting—the serenity of being home.

Realistically, I know that life takes a jagged course. In one recent season alone, tragedy, sadness, and illness threatened my serenity like a masked invader at the door. Every few days, contemporaries appeared in the obituaries, grandkids got hurt "getting air" on skis, bikes, or skateboards, looking for more and more dangerous thrills. Mel had a heart attack on Christmas morning, needed stents in his blocked vessels. A daughter went through an agonizing divorce, loved ones battled with genetic compulsions, granddaughters struggled with decisions to marry and treatments to get pregnant. Jobs were elusive, friends suffered terminal illness, a flu bug decided to take up residence in my lungs.

On a giant scale, war and pestilence, environmental calamities, starvation, and inhumanities can seem to outweigh the goodness in a world so often gone awry. God can seem, to many, uncaring and inaccessible, if not nonexistent. But for my own journey, I can keep alive my very real knowing that relief will come, that God reaches my reaching, that the small glories will prevail.

For my eightieth birthday, my family gave me a surprise tennis party. Three daughters took me to our old Salt Lake Tennis Club for what I thought would be the blood-battle doubles we play on girls' trips. But, from behind the back curtains, popped thirty-nine of my family—kids and grandkids, brothers and sisters-in-law, and one longtime tennis friend, ready for the "Grandma Grey Grand Slam." Tennis pro son-in-law Mike had a draw with everyone playing with everyone, the whole place running with relatives.

Dinner was upstairs with medals for teams and a trophy for me engraved with "Happy 80th" and Father's motto, "Try hard, play fair, have fun." Great-grandkids, all under the age of four, made everyone laugh. A poem by a daughter and a half-hour video of my dears talking about me made me cry, and Mel too. Our daughters played their violins, piano, and flute—"Love at Home" and "Movin' On"—that they'd played for me since they were small. I thought, "Why not turn eighty every year? What a dream! Lucky lady, Lulie."

And I remembered that poem of ten years ago about the dandelion. How many nanoseconds since? How many till a final journey to the place of knowing? I'll be sure to pay close attention.

They have scattered, the small glories that outwit the disasters. In either my life at home or away, I am blessed with knowing that by paying attention, any place or time can be part of a spiritual journey that is much more than a trip toward getting old.

I AM DELIGHTED

I am delighted. My life goes well.
I must say it as clearly as I can
before I'm gone.
So little delight there can seem in the world.
Almost as if it's shameful or naive
to love what is there:

a new collapsible pair of glasses
flat in a one-inch pouch—imagine!
Can be worn inside my bra:
anywhere the telephone book,
a needle, newsprint—it's OK.
Touch a key on my new computer:
Clean up window. *And tiny icons*
on a desktop scoot about for space—
alphabetical!

Take a 4 o'clock walk
from Sun Valley to Ketchum
past the fields and watch a young mare
and gelding frolicking like kittens,
a nine-year-old biker trying to look nonchalant
as he sails past
with no hands.
Hear the brook getting in with
the white swans at the black pond.
Feel the sun making its last statement
to the fence posts.
Smell the perfume of the yellow-haired
lady strolling with her hand in the short man's hand.
Nod as the civilized gives way

to the languid redolence
of manure.

Back, find the word I've hunted for:
forage, jasmine, medallion.
Taste the strawberries on yogurt
at my own sink.
Let the shower have its way with
my hair.
Be tired.
After they have stood and sat and walked
and climbed the stairs, put those legs
to bed.
Talk not at all.
Take as long as I need
to find the fit.
And those eyes, let them close.
See, see, particles of delight
to sleep with
and be delightfully surprised by
tomorrow.

EPILOGUE

Twenty-four years have passed since my accident and experience with death. This book has had a difficult journey. Keeping my promises has been even more difficult. Days and nights are still, at eighty-six, full of too many and too much, mostly of my own choosing. Still, I feel lucky to have the choices.

Spiritual perception in the real world is tricky. The reality of life gets in the way of living in the spirit—it's hard to stay there. Writing about it is easier than living it. My mentor, friend, and spiritual leader, Dr. Lowell L. Bennion, inspired me to stay in touch vertically with the divine and horizontally with the human. His teachings included:

Call on the Lord.
Consider the overall benefit.
Overcome evil with good.
Tell the devil to go to hell.
Keep your integrity.
Be an actor, not a reactor.
Be responsible for finding the full measure of your creation.
Act out of love, not fear or grievance.
Speak with your own voice and write with your own pen.
Whatever you do, do with joy and with faith.

This all is encompassed in Psalm 139:1–14

O Lord, thou hast searched me, and known me.

Thou knowest my downsitting and mine uprising, thou
understandest my thoughts afar off.

Thou compassest my path and my lying down and art
acquainted with all my ways.

For there is not a word in my tongue, but, lo, O Lord, thou
knowest it altogether.

Thou has beset me behind and before, and laid thine hand
upon me.

Such knowledge is too wonderful for me; it is high, I cannot
attain unto it.

Whither shall I go from thy spirit? or whither shall I flee from
thy presence?

If I ascend up into heaven, thou art there: if I make my bed in
hell, behold thou art there.

If I take the wings of the morning, and dwell in the uttermost
parts of the sea;

Even there shall thy hand lead me, and thy right hand shall
hold me.

If I say, Surely the darkness shall cover me; even the night shall
be light about me.

Yea, the darkness hideth not from thee; but the night shineth as
the day;

The darkness and the light are both alike to thee.

For thou hast possessed my reins: thou hast covered me in my
mother's womb.

I will praise thee; for I am fearfully and wonderfully made:
marvelous are thy works; and that my soul knoweth right
well.

I must accept that I'll make my spiritual life work as best I can—
to bring depth and meaning to life even now and then, loving each
other however it works.

GLOSSARY

Apostle—One of the twelve highest general authorities in the Mormon Church

Bishop—Leader of a ward

Book of Mormon—Companion to the Bible, a testament of Christ revealing the history of ancient people on the American continent, translated by Joseph Smith

Celestial Room—Most sacred room in a temple where members meditate following the performance of ordinances, such as marriages

Deacon—First level of priesthood for boys age twelve to fourteen; may pass the sacrament to all members at Sunday meeting

Elder—Fourth level of priesthood for young men age nineteen and older; may serve as a proselytizing missionary

First Presidency—Top three officers in the Mormon Church

General Authority—A leader of the Mormon Church, directly under the president

General Board—A group of members called to lead a worldwide auxiliary: Primary, Young Women, Young Men, Sunday School, and Relief Society

General Conference—A three-day, semiannual meeting in the Conference Center in Salt Lake City, seating 20,000 and broadcast worldwide; speakers are general authorities of the church

Joseph Smith—Founder and first prophet of the Church of Jesus Christ of Latter-day Saints (Mormon)

Moroni—Angel who appeared to Joseph Smith as a young boy; Angel Moroni statue is atop every Mormon temple

President—Top leader and prophet of the Mormon Church

Priest—Third level of priesthood for young men age sixteen to eighteen; may offer a prayer to bless the sacrament at Sunday meeting

Priesthood—Holy authority of ordained adult male members of the Mormon Church to preside at meetings, baptize, marry, and give blessings to heal

Primary—Organization for teaching children ages three to twelve

Prophet—Senior apostle; president and receiver of revelations for the Mormon Church

Relief Society—The serving and learning organization for adult women

Roll—Record of attendance at various meetings

Sacrament—Holy bread and water served in remembrance of Christ's sacrifice

Sacrament Meeting—Held on Sunday for all members: sermons are delivered by lay members; sacrament is passed by deacons to all in the congregation

Tabernacle—Largest hall on Temple Square in Salt Lake City; seats 4,000; home of the Mormon Tabernacle Choir, broadcasting every Sunday morning since 1929—no regular meetings held there

Temple—Building where sacred ordinances are performed, such as baptisms and marriages; no congregational meetings are held there (approximately 140 worldwide)

Temple Clothes—Special white clothing considered sacred and to be worn only in the temple

Testimony—Expressed belief in the divine and/or the church, delivered by church members in many settings, including spontaneously in a monthly sacrament meeting following a twenty-four hour fast

Ward—A congregation of worshipers defined by geographical boundaries (usually about 300 families who meet together regularly); also the building housing all activities—meetings and funerals in the chapel; classrooms for teaching; a recreation hall for dinners, sports, and wedding receptions; a nursery for children ages eighteen months to three years

Welfare Plan—Worldwide assistance to members or nonmembers in need, providing food, clothing, medical and emergency supplies; sponsored by donations, tithing, and fast offerings (the cost of two missed meals)

Word of Wisdom—Prescribed dietary and health code, including abstinence from liquor, tobacco, drugs, tea, and coffee

CPSIA information can be obtained at www.ICGtesting.com
Printed in the USA
268238BV00002B/31/P